Professional Resumes Series

RESUMES
FOR
BUSINESS
MANAGEMENT
CAREERS

The Editors of
VGM Career Books

Second Edition

VGM Career Books
NTC/Contemporary Publishing Group

Library of Congress Cataloging-in-Publication Data

Resumes for business management careers / [compiled and edited by]
Jeffrey S. Johnson—2nd. ed.
     p. cm.—(VGM professional resumes series)
    ISBN 0-658-00455-7
    1. Resumes—(Employment)   2. Cover letters.
    3. Executives—United States.
    I. Johnson, Jeffrey S.   II. Series
HF5383.V46   2000
808'.06665—dc21   00-38188
                                        CIP

The editors gratefully acknowledge Jeffrey S. Johnson for his help in the writing and production of this book.

Interior design by City Desktop Productions

Published by VGM Career Books
A division of NTC/Contemporary Publishing Group, Inc.
4255 West Touhy Avenue, Lincolnwood (Chicago), Illinois 60712-1975 U.S.A.
Printed in the United States of America
International Standard Book Number: 0-658-00455-7
00 01 02 03 04 VL 15 14 13 12 11 10 9 8 7 6 5 4 3 2 1

Contents

Introduction

Your resume is your first impression on a prospective employer. Though you may be articulate, intelligent, and charming in person, a poor resume may prevent you from ever having the opportunity to demonstrate your interpersonal skills, because a poor resume may prevent you from ever being called for an interview. While few people have ever been hired solely on the basis of their resume, a well-written, well-organized resume can go a long way toward helping you land an interview. Your resume's main purpose is to get you that interview. The rest is up to you and the employer. If you both feel that you are right for the job and the job is right for you, chances are you will be hired.

A resume must catch the reader's attention yet still be easy to read and to the point. Resume styles have changed over the years. Today, brief and focused resumes are preferred. No longer do employers have the patience, or the time, to review several pages of solid type. A resume should be only one page long, if possible. Time is a precious commodity in today's business world, and the resume that is concise and straightforward will usually be the one that gets noticed.

Let's not make the mistake, though, of assuming that writing a brief resume means that you can take less care in preparing it. A successful resume takes time and thought, and if you are willing to make the effort, the rewards are well worth it. Think of your resume as a sales tool with the product being you. You want to sell yourself to a prospective employer. This book is designed to help you prepare a resume that will further your career—to land that next job, or first job, or to return to the workforce after years of absence. So, read on. Make the effort and reap the rewards that a strong resume can bring to your career. Let's get to it!

The Elements of a Good Resume

A winning resume is made of the elements that employers are most interested in seeing when reviewing a job applicant. These basic elements are the essential ingredients of a successful resume and become the actual sections of your resume. The following is a list of elements that may be used in a resume. Some are essential, some are optional. We will be discussing these in this chapter to give you a better understanding of each element's role in the makeup of your resume:

1. Heading
2. Objective
3. Work Experience
4. Education
5. Honors
6. Activities
7. Certificates and Licenses
8. Professional Memberships
9. Special Skills
10. Personal Information
11. References

The first step in preparing your resume is to gather information about yourself and your past accomplishments. Later you will refine this information, rewrite it in the most effective language, and organize it into the most attractive layout. First, let's take a look at each of these important elements individually.

Heading

The heading may seem to be a simple enough element in your resume, but be careful not to take it lightly. The heading should be placed at the top of your resume and should include your name, home address, and telephone numbers. If you can take calls at your current place of business, include your business number, since most employers will attempt to contact you during the business day. If this is not possible, or if you can afford it, purchase an answering machine that allows you to retrieve your messages while you are away from home. This way you can make sure you don't miss important phone calls. Always include your phone number on your resume. It is crucial that when prospective employers need to have immediate contact with you, they can.

Objective

When seeking a particular career path, it is important to list a job objective on your resume. This statement helps employers know the direction that you see yourself heading, so that they can determine whether your goals are in line with the position available. The objective is normally one sentence long and describes your employment goals clearly and concisely. See the sample resumes in this book for examples of objective statements.

The job objective will vary depending on the type of person you are, the field you are in, and the type of goals you have. It can be either specific or general, but it should always be to the point.

In some cases, this element is not necessary, but usually it is a good idea to include your objective. It gives your possible future employer an idea of where you are coming from and where you want to go.

The objective statement is better left out, however, if you are uncertain of the exact title of the job you seek. In such a case, the inclusion of an overly specific objective statement could result in your not being considered for a variety of acceptable positions; be sure to incorporate this information in your cover letter instead.

Work Experience

This element is arguably the most important of them all. It will provide the central focus of your resume, so it is necessary that this section be as complete as possible. Only by examining your work experience in depth can you get to the heart of your accomplishments and present them in a way that demonstrates the strength of your qualifications. Of course, someone just out of school will have less work experience than someone who has been working for a number of years, but the amount of information isn't the most important thing—rather, how it is presented, and how it highlights you as a person and as a worker will be what counts.

As you work on this section of your resume, be aware of the need for accuracy. You'll want to include all necessary information about each of your jobs, including job title, dates, employer, city, state, responsibilities, special projects, and accomplishments. Be sure to only list company accomplishments for which you were directly responsible. If you haven't participated in any special projects, that's all right—this area may not be relevant to certain jobs.

The most common way to list your work experience is in *reverse chronological order*. In other words, start with your most recent job and work your way backward. This way your prospective employer sees your current (and often most important) job before seeing your past jobs. Your most recent position, if the most important, should also be the one that includes the most information, as compared to your previous positions. If you are just out of school, show your summer employment and part-time work, though in this case your education will most likely be more important than your work experience.

The following worksheets will help you gather information about your past jobs.

WORK EXPERIENCE

Job One:

Job Title _____

Dates _____

Employer _____

City, State _____

Major Duties _____

_____

_____

_____

_____

_____

_____

_____

_____

Special Projects _____

_____

_____

_____

Accomplishments _____

_____

_____

_____

_____

_____

_____

_____

Job Two:

Job Title _____

Dates _____

Employer _____

City, State _____

Major Duties _____

_____

_____

_____

_____

_____

_____

_____

Special Projects _____

_____

_____

_____

Accomplishments _____

_____

_____

_____

_____

_____

_____

_____

Job Three:

Job Title _____

Dates _____

Employer _____

City, State _____

Major Duties _____

_____

_____

_____

_____

_____

_____

_____

Special Projects _____

_____

_____

_____

Accomplishments _____

_____

_____

_____

_____

_____

_____

_____

Job Four:

Job Title _____

Dates _____

Employer _____

City, State _____

Major Duties _____

_____

_____

_____

_____

_____

_____

_____

Special Projects _____

_____

_____

_____

Accomplishments _____

_____

_____

_____

_____

_____

_____

_____

Education

Education is the second most important element of a resume. Your educational background is often a deciding factor in an employer's decision to hire you. Be sure to stress your accomplishments in school with the same finesse that you stressed your accomplishments at work. If you are looking for your first job, your education will be your greatest asset, since your work experience will most likely be minimal. In this case, the education section becomes the most important. You will want to be sure to include any degrees or certificates you received, your major area of concentration, any honors, and any relevant activities. Again, be sure to list your most recent schooling first. If you have completed graduate-level work, begin with that and work in reverse chronological order through your undergraduate education. If you have completed an undergraduate degree, you may choose whether to list your high school experience or not. This should be done only if your high school grade point average was well above average.

The following worksheets will help you gather information for this section of your resume. Also included are supplemental worksheets for honors and for activities. Sometimes honors and activities are listed in a section separate from education, most often near the end of the resume.

EDUCATION

School One _____

Major or Area of Concentration _____

Degree _____

Dates _____

School Two _____

Major or Area of Concentration _____

Degree _____

Dates _____

Honors

Here you should list any awards, honors, or memberships in honorary societies that you have received. Usually these are of an academic nature, but they can also be for special achievement in sports, clubs, or other school activities. Always be sure to include the name of the organization honoring you and the date(s) received. Use the worksheet below to help gather your honors information.

HONORS

Honor One _____

Awarding Organization _____

Date(s) _____

Honor Two _____

Awarding Organization _____

Date(s) _____

Honor Three _____

Awarding Organization _____

Date(s) _____

Honor Four _____

Awarding Organization _____

Date(s) _____

Activities

You may have been active in different organizations or clubs during your years at school; often an employer will look at such involvement as evidence of initiative and dedication. Your ability to take an active role, and even a leadership role, in a group should be included on your resume. Use the worksheet provided to list your activities and accomplishments in this area. In general, you should exclude any organization whose name indicates the race, creed, sex, age, marital status, color, or nation of origin of its members.

ACTIVITIES

Organization/Activity _____

Accomplishments _____

_____

_____

Organization/Activity _____

Accomplishments _____

_____

_____

Organization/Activity _____

Accomplishments _____

_____

_____

Organization/Activity _____

Accomplishments _____

_____

_____

As your work experience increases through the years, your school activities and honors will play less of a role in your resume, and eventually you will most likely only list your degree and any major honors you received. This is due to the fact that, as time goes by, your job performance becomes the most important element in your resume. Through time, your resume should change to reflect this.

Certificates and Licenses

The next potential element of your resume is certificates and licenses. You should list these if the job you are seeking requires them and you, of course, have acquired them. If you have applied for a license, but have not yet received it, use the phrase "application pending."

License requirements vary by state. If you have moved or are planning to move to another state, be sure to check with that state's board or licensing agency for all licensing requirements.

Always be sure that all of the information you list is completely accurate. Locate copies of your licenses and certificates and check the exact date and name of the accrediting agency. Use the following worksheet to list your licenses and certificates.

CERTIFICATES AND LICENSES

Name of License _____

Licensing Agency _____

Date Issued _____

Name of License _____

Licensing Agency _____

Date Issued _____

Name of License _____

Licensing Agency _____

Date Issued _____

Professional Memberships

Another potential element in your resume is a section listing professional memberships. Use this section to list involvement in professional associations, unions, and similar organizations. It is to your advantage to list any professional memberships that pertain to the job you are seeking. Be sure to include the dates of your involvement and whether you took part in any special activities or held any offices within the organization. Use the following worksheet to gather your information.

PROFESSIONAL MEMBERSHIPS

Name of Organization _____

Offices Held _____

Activities _____

Dates _____

Name of Organization _____

Offices Held _____

Activities _____

Dates _____

Name of Organization _____

Offices Held _____

Activities _____

Dates _____

Name of Organization _____

Offices Held _____

Activities _____

Dates _____

Special Skills

This section of your resume is for mentioning any special abilities you have that could relate to the job you are seeking. This is the part of your resume where you have the opportunity to demonstrate certain talents and experiences that are not necessarily a part of your educational or work experience. Common examples include fluency in a foreign language or knowledge of a particular computer application.

Special skills can encompass a wide range of your talents—remember that whatever skills you list should relate to the type of work you are looking for.

Personal Information

Some people include "Personal" information on their resumes. This is not generally recommended, but you might wish to include it if you think that something in your personal life, such as a hobby or talent, has some bearing on the position you are seeking. This type of information is often referred to at the beginning of an interview, when it is used as an "ice breaker." Of course, personal information regarding age, marital status, race, religion, or sexual preference should never appear on any resume.

References

References are not usually listed on the resume, but a prospective employer needs to know that you have references who may be contacted if necessary. All that is necessary to include in your resume regarding references is a sentence at the bottom stating, "References are available upon request." If a prospective employer requests a list of references, be sure to have one ready. Also, check with whomever you list to see if it is all right for you to use them as a reference. Forewarn them that they may receive a call regarding a reference for you. This way they can be prepared to give you the best reference possible.

Writing Your Resume

Now that you have gathered all of the information for each of the sections of your resume, it's time to write out each section in a way that will get the attention of whoever is reviewing it. The type of language you use in your resume will affect its success. You want to take the information you have gathered and translate it into a language that will cause a potential employer to sit up and take notice.

Resume writing is not like expository writing or creative writing. It embodies a functional, direct writing style and focuses on the use of action words. By using action words in your writing, you more effectively stress past accomplishments. Action words demonstrate your initiative and highlight your talents. Always use verbs that show strength and reflect the qualities of a "doer." By using action words, you characterize yourself as a person who takes action, and this will impress potential employers.

The following is a list of verbs commonly used in resume writing. Use this list to choose the action words that can help your resume become a strong one:

administered	billed
advised	built
analyzed	carried out
arranged	channeled
assembled	collected
assumed responsibility	communicated

compiled	maintained
completed	managed
conducted	met with
contacted	motivated
contracted	negotiated
coordinated	operated
counseled	orchestrated
created	ordered
cut	organized
designed	oversaw
determined	performed
developed	planned
directed	prepared
dispatched	presented
distributed	produced
documented	programmed
edited	published
established	purchased
expanded	recommended
functioned as	recorded
gathered	reduced
handled	referred
hired	represented
implemented	researched
improved	reviewed
inspected	saved
interviewed	screened
introduced	served as
invented	served on

sold	tested
suggested	trained
supervised	typed
taught	wrote

Now take a look at the information you put down on the work experience worksheets. Take that information and rewrite it in paragraph form, using verbs to highlight your actions and accomplishments. Let's look at an example, remembering that what matters here is the writing style, and not the particular job responsibilities given in our sample.

WORK EXPERIENCE
Regional Sales Manager

Manager of sales representatives from seven states. Responsible for twelve food chain accounts in the East. In charge of directing the sales force in planned selling toward specific goals. Supervisor and trainer of new sales representatives. Consulting for customers in the areas of inventory management and quality control.

Special Projects: Coordinator and sponsor of annual food industry sales seminar.

Accomplishments: Monthly regional volume went up 25 percent during my tenure while, at the same time, a proper sales/cost ratio was maintained. Customer/company relations improved significantly.

Below is the rewritten version of this information, using action words. Notice how much stronger it sounds.

WORK EXPERIENCE
Regional Sales Manager

Managed sales representatives from seven states. Handled twelve food chain accounts in the eastern United States. Directed the sales force in planned selling toward specific goals. Supervised and trained new sales representatives. Consulted for customers in the areas of inventory management and quality control. Coordinated and sponsored the annual Food Industry Seminar. Increased monthly regional volume 25 percent and helped to improve customer/company relations during my tenure.

Another way of constructing the work experience section is by using actual job descriptions. Job descriptions are rarely written using the proper resume language, but they do include all the information necessary to create this section of your resume. Take the description of one of the jobs you are including on your resume (if you have access to it), and turn it into an action-oriented paragraph. Below is an example of a job description followed by a version of the same description written using action words. Again, pay attention to the style of writing, as the details of your own work experience will be unique.

WORK EXPERIENCE
Public Administrator I

Responsibilities: Coordinate and direct public services to meet the needs of the nation, state, or community. Analyze problems; work with special committees and public agencies; recommend solutions to governing bodies.

Aptitudes and Skills: Ability to relate to and communicate with people; solve complex problems through analysis; plan, organize, and implement policies and programs. Knowledge of political systems; financial management; personnel administration; program evaluation; organizational theory.

WORK EXPERIENCE
Public Administrator I

Wrote pamphlets and conducted discussion groups to inform citizens of legislative processes and consumer issues. Organized and supervised 25 interviewers. Trained interviewers in effective communication skills.

Now that you have learned how to word your resume, you are ready for the next step in your quest for a winning resume: assembly and layout.

Chapter 3

Assembly and Layout

At this point, you've gathered all the necessary information for your resume, and you've rewritten it using the language necessary to impress potential employers. Your next step is to assemble these elements in a logical order and lay them out on the page neatly and attractively to achieve the desired effect: getting that interview.

Assembly

The order of the elements in a resume makes a difference in its overall effect. Obviously, you would not want to put your name and address in the middle of the resume or your special skills section at the top. You want to put the elements in an order that stresses your most important achievements, not the less pertinent information. For example, if you recently graduated from school and have no full-time work experience, you will want to list your education before you list any part-time jobs you may have held during school. On the other hand, if you have been gainfully employed for several years and currently hold an important position in your company, you will want to list your work experience ahead of your education, which has become less pertinent with time.

There are some elements that are always included in your resume and some that are optional. Following is a list of essential and optional elements:

Essential	Optional
Name	Job Objective
Address	Honors
Phone Number	Special Skills
Work Experience	Professional Memberships
Education	Activities
References Phrase	Certificates and Licenses
	Personal Information

Your choice of optional sections depends on your own background and employment needs. Always use information that puts you and your abilities in a favorable light. If your honors are impressive, then be sure to include them in your resume. If your activities in school demonstrate particular talents necessary for the job you are seeking, then allow space for a section on activities. Each resume is unique, just as each person is unique.

Types of Resumes

So far, our discussion about resumes has involved the most common type—the *reverse chronological* resume, in which your most recent job is listed first and so on. This is the type of resume usually preferred by human resources directors, and it is the one most frequently used. However, in some cases this style of presentation is not the most effective way to highlight your skills and accomplishments.

For someone reentering the workforce after many years or someone looking to change career fields, the *functional resume* may work best. This type of resume focuses more on achievement and less on the sequence of your work history. In the functional resume, your experience is presented by what you have accomplished and the skills you have developed in your past work.

A functional resume can be assembled from the same information you collected for your chronological resume. The main difference lies in how you organize this information. Essentially, the work experience section becomes two sections, with your job duties and accomplishments comprising one section and your employer's name, city, state, your position, and the dates employed making up another section. The first section is placed near the top of the resume, just below the job objective section, and can be called *Accomplishments* or *Achievements*. The second section, containing the bare essentials of your employment history, should come after the accomplishments section and can be titled *Work Experience* or *Employment History*. The other sections of your resume remain the same. The work experience section is the only one affected in the functional resume. By placing the section that focuses on your achievements first, you draw attention to these achievements. This puts less emphasis on who you worked for and more emphasis on what you did and what you are capable of doing.

For someone changing careers, emphasis on skills and achievements is essential. The identities of previous employers, which may be unrelated to one's new job field, need to be downplayed. The functional resume accomplishes this task. For someone reentering the workforce after many years, a functional resume is the obvious choice. If you lack full-time work experience, you will need to draw attention away from this fact and instead focus on your skills and abilities gained possibly through volunteer activities or part-time work. Education may also play a more important role in this resume.

Which type of resume is right for you depends on your own personal circumstances. It may be helpful to create a chronological and a functional resume and then compare the two to find out which is more suitable. The sample resumes found in this book include both chronological and functional resumes. Use these resumes as guides to help you decide on the content and appearance of your own resume.

Layout

Once you have decided which elements to include in your resume and you have arranged them in an order that makes sense and emphasizes your achievements and abilities, then it is time to work on the physical layout of your resume.

There is no single appropriate layout that applies to every resume, but there are a few basic rules to follow in putting your resume on paper:

1. Leave a comfortable margin on the sides, top, and bottom of the page (usually 1 to 1½ inches).

2. Use appropriate spacing between the sections (usually 2 to 3 line spaces are adequate).

3. Be consistent in the *type* of headings you use for the different sections of your resume. For example, if you capitalize the heading EMPLOYMENT HISTORY, don't use initial capitals and underlining for a heading of equal importance, such as Education.

CHRONOLOGICAL RESUME

DAVID P. JENKINS

3663 N. Coldwater Canyon • North Hollywood, CA 90390
818/555-3472 • 818/555-3678

JOB OBJECTIVE

A position as a sales/marketing manager where I can use my knowledge and experience by combining high-volume selling of major accounts with an administrative ability that increases sales through encouragement of sales team.

EMPLOYMENT HISTORY

Tribor Industries, Los Angeles, CA
Regional Sales Manager, 1993 - present

Managed sales of all product lines in western markets for a leading maker of linens. Represented five corporate divisions of the company with sales in excess of $3,000,000 annually. Directed and motivated a sales force of 12 sales representatives in planned selling to achieve company goals.

Tribor Industries, Los Angeles, CA
District Manager, 1988 - 1993

Acted as sales representative for the Los Angeles metropolitan area. Built both wholesale and dealer distribution substantially during my tenure. Promoted to Regional Manager after five years of service.

American Office Supply, Chicago, IL
Assistant Sales Manager, 1984 - 1988

Handled both internal and external sales and marketing, including samples, advertising, and pricing. Served as company sales representative and sold a variety of office supplies to retail stores.

EDUCATION

University of Michigan, Ann Arbor, MI
B.A. Business Administration, 1983
Major Field: Management

SEMINARS

National Management Association Seminar, 1992
Purdue University Seminars, 1995, 1997

PROFESSIONAL MEMBERSHIPS

Sales and Marketing Association of Los Angeles
National Association of Market Developers

REFERENCES

Available upon request.

FUNCTIONAL RESUME

Sara Woods
4400 Sunset Blvd., Los Angeles, CA 90028
(213) 555-8989 • (213) 555-4950

Objective
A position in sales management.

Achievements
- Planned successful strategies to identify and develop new accounts.
- Increased sales by at least 20 percent each year as District Sales Manager.
- Researched and analyzed market conditions in order to seek out new customers.
- Developed weekly and monthly sales strategies.
- Supervised seven sales representatives.
- Conducted field visits to solve customer complaints.
- Maintained daily customer contact to ensure good customer/company relations.
- Wrote product information flyers and distributed them through a direct-mail program.

Work Experience
Southern California Fruit Co.
Los Angeles, CA
District Sales Manager, 1994 - present

L.A. Freight Co.
Los Angeles, CA
Account Executive, 1992 - 1994

Handlemen & Associates
Santa Rita, CA
Sales Representative, 1991 - 1992

Education
University of Colorado, Boulder, CO
B.A., 1991
Major: Management
Minor: Political Science
G.P.A.: 3.3/4.0

Professional Memberships
- Southern California Sales Association, Treasurer, 1996 - 1998
- Los Angeles Chamber of Commerce, 1994 - present

Special Skills
- Experienced with Lotus and WordPerfect.

References
Provided on request.

4. Always try to fit your resume onto one page. If you are having trouble fitting all your information onto one page, perhaps you are trying to say too much. Edit out any repetitive or unnecessary information or shorten descriptions of earlier jobs. Be ruthless. Maybe you've included too many optional sections.

Don't let the idea of having to tell every detail about your life get in the way of producing a resume that is simple and straightforward. The more compact your resume, the easier it is to read and the better an impression it will make for you.

In some cases, the resume will not fit on a single page, even after extensive editing. In such cases, the resume should be printed on two pages so as not to compromise clarity or appearance. Each page of a two-page resume should be marked clearly with your name and the page number, for example, "Judith Ramirez, page 1 of 2." The pages should be stapled together.

Experiment with various layouts until you find one that looks good to you. Always show your final layout to other people and ask them what they like or dislike about it, and what impresses them most about your resume. Make sure that is what you want most to emphasize. If it isn't, you may want to consider making changes in your layout until the necessary information is emphasized. Use the sample resumes in this book to get some ideas for laying out your resume.

Putting Your Resume in Print

Your resume should be typed or printed on good quality $8\frac{1}{2}'' \times 11''$ bond paper. You want to make as good an impression as possible with your resume; therefore, quality paper is a necessity. If you have access to a word processor with a good printer, or know of someone who does, make use of it. Typewritten resumes should only be used when there are no other options available.

After you have produced a clean original, make duplicate copies of it. Usually a copy shop is your best bet for producing copies without smudges or streaks. Make sure you have the copy shop use quality bond paper for all copies of your resume. Ask for a sample copy before they run your entire order. After copies are made, check each copy for cleanliness and clarity.

Another more costly option is to have your resume typeset and printed by a printer. This provides the most attractive resume of all. If you anticipate needing a lot of copies of your resume, the cost of having it typeset may be justified.

Proofreading

After you have finished typing the master copy of your resume and before you have it copied or printed, thoroughly check it for typing and spelling errors. Have several people read it over just in case you have missed an error. Misspelled words and typing mistakes do not make a good impression on a prospective employer, as they are a bad reflection on your writing ability and your attention to detail. With thorough and conscientious proofreading, these mistakes can be avoided.

The following are some rules of capitalization and punctuation that may come in handy when proofreading your resume:

RULES OF CAPITALIZATION

- Capitalize proper nouns, such as names of schools, colleges, and universities; names of companies; and brand names of products.

- Capitalize major words in the names and titles of books, tests, and articles that appear in the body of your resume.

- Capitalize words in major section headings of your resume.

- Do not capitalize words just because they seem important.

- When in doubt, consult a manual of style such as *Words into Type* (Prentice Hall), or *The Chicago Manual of Style* (The University of Chicago Press). Your local library can help you locate these and other reference books.

RULES OF PUNCTUATION

- Use a comma to separate words in a series.

- Use a semicolon to separate series of words that already include commas within the series.

- Use a semicolon to separate independent clauses that are not joined by a conjunction.

- Use a period to end a sentence.

- Use a colon to show that examples or details follow that will expand or amplify the preceding phrase.

- Avoid the use of dashes.

- Avoid the use of brackets.

- If you use any punctuation in an unusual way in your resume, be consistent in its use.

- Whenever you are uncertain, consult a style manual.

Chapter 4

The Cover Letter

Once your resume has been assembled, laid out, and printed to your satisfaction, the next step before distribution is to write your cover letter. Though there may be instances when you deliver your resume in person, you usually send it through the mail. Resumes sent through the mail always need an accompanying letter that briefly introduces you and your resume. The purpose of the cover letter is to get a potential employer to read your resume, just as the purpose of your resume is to get that same potential employer to call you for an interview.

Like your resume, your cover letter should be clean, neat, and direct. A cover letter usually includes the following information:

1. Your name and address (unless it already appears on your personal letterhead).

2. The date.

3. The name and address of the person and company to whom you are sending your resume.

4. The salutation ("Dear Mr." or "Dear Ms." followed by the person's last name, or "To Whom It May Concern" if you are answering a blind ad).

5. An opening paragraph explaining why you are writing (in response to an ad, the result of a previous meeting, at the suggestion of someone you both know) and indicating that you are interested in whatever job is being offered.

6. One or two more paragraphs that tell why you want to work for the company and what qualifications and experience you can bring to that company.

7. A final paragraph that closes the letter and requests that you be contacted for an interview.

8. The closing ("Sincerely," or "Yours truly," followed by your signature with your name typed under it).

Your cover letter, including all of the information above, should be no more than one page in length. The language used should be polite, businesslike, and to the point. Do not attempt to tell your life story in the cover letter. A long and cluttered letter will only serve to put off the reader. Remember, you only need to mention a few of your accomplishments and skills in the cover letter. The rest of your information is in your resume. Every achievement should not be mentioned twice. If your cover letter is a success, your resume will be read and all pertinent information reviewed by your prospective employer.

Producing the Cover Letter

Cover letters should always be individualized, since they are always written to particular individuals and companies. Never use a form letter for your cover letter. Cover letters cannot be copied or reproduced like resumes. Each one should be as personal as possible. Of course, once you have written and rewritten your first cover letter to the point where you are satisfied with it, you can use similar wording in subsequent letters.

After you have typed your cover letter on quality bond paper, proofread it as thoroughly as you did your resume. Again, spelling errors are a sure sign of carelessness, and you don't want that to be a part of your first impression on a prospective employer. Handle the letter and resume carefully to avoid any smudges, and then mail both your cover letter and resume in an appropriately sized envelope. Keep an accurate record of all the resumes you send out and the results of each mailing, either in a separate notebook or on individual index cards.

Numerous sample cover letters appear at the end of this book. Use them as models for your own cover letter or to get an idea of how cover letters are put together. Remember, every cover letter is unique and depends on the particular circumstances of the individual writing it and the job for which he or she is applying.

Now the job of writing your resume and cover letter is complete. About a week after mailing resumes and cover letters to potential employers, contact them by telephone. Confirm that your resume arrived, and ask whether an interview might be possible. Getting your foot in the door during this call is half the battle of a job search, and a strong resume and cover letter will help you immeasurably.

Chapter 5

Sample Resumes

This chapter contains dozens of sample resumes for people pursuing a wide variety of jobs and careers within this field.

There are many different styles of resumes in terms of graphic layout and presentation of information. These samples also represent people with varying amounts of education and work experience. Use these samples to model your own resume after. Choose one resume or borrow elements from several different resumes to help you construct your own.

BARRY SCRANT

111 Willoughby Road #3
Parkview, SD 30039
605/555-2212

OBJECTIVE

A job in personnel administration leading to personnel management.

SKILLS & EXPERIENCE

Interviewed 50 South Dakota farmers for senior research project, *The South Dakota Farm Industry: Boom or Bust?* Collected and analyzed data. Developed a questionnaire.

Served as a student representative on the university's planning committee. Worked on a subcommittee that dealt with policy formulation.

Wrote the article "South Dakota's Future" for the *South Dakota News*, October 1998.

Collected and analyzed statistical data on local Farm Union elections.

EDUCATION

Jefferson University, Parkview, SD

B.A. in Sociology, 1999

Areas of concentration included: employee relations, psychology, communications.

REFERENCES PROVIDED ON REQUEST.

ANTONIO MARINO
8900 Santa Monica Blvd. #880
Los Angeles, CA 90069
213/555-4098

OBJECTIVE

A management position in the field of finance.

EDUCATION

UCLA, Los Angeles, CA
Graduate School of Business Administration
M.B.A. expected June 2000
Concentration: Finance
Finance Club
Student Advisory Board

Northwestern University, Evanston, IL
B.A. in Economics, 1997
Summa Cum Laude
Phi Beta Kappa
Student Government Vice President

WORK EXPERIENCE

Marshall & Thompson, Los Angeles, CA
Financial Accounting Intern, 1999
Participated in standard accounting, credit approval, budgeting, and variance analysis.
Handled bank balances and money management.

Wells Fargo Bank, Los Angeles, CA
Commercial Loan Intern, 1998
Oversaw accounts in the automated teller system. Provided financial data to commercial
account officers. Handled the collection of arrears.

Northwestern University, Evanston, IL
Assistant, Accounts Payable Department, 1996 - 1997
Assisted with bookkeeping, check requests, and disbursements. Billed invoices. Tracked
accounts receivable and accounts payable.

REFERENCES

Available upon request.

ANGELICA USTIN
19999 S. Main St.
Birmingham, AL 33909
205/555-2289
austin22@aol.com

POSITION DESIRED: *Assistant Manager of a women's clothing boutique.*

EXPERIENCE: *Retail*
- Assisted customers in making selections.
- Handled customer complaints and exchanges.
- Oversaw promotional events and publicity.
- Designed window and counter displays.
- Contributed to store website.

Bookkeeping
- Handled accounts payable and receivable.
- Processed invoices.
- Maintained ledger.
- Balanced daily receipts with register funds.
- Prepared financial statements.

EMPLOYMENT HISTORY: *Georgia's Boutique, Birmingham, AL*
Assistant Manager, 1995 - present

Jovan's, Westport, AL
Salesperson, 1992 - 1995

Thrifty Drug, Birmingham, AL
Cashier, 1990 - 1992

EDUCATION: *Birmingham Junior College, Birmingham, AL*
Attended 1989
Area of Concentration: Accounting

Shawanee High School, Reed, AL
Graduated 1988
Student Council
Poetry Club

REFERENCES: *Available on request.*

STEPHANIE SHEPARD

804 N. Victoria Park Rd.

Ft. Myers, FL 30013

813/555-2000 (Work)

813/555-5555 (Home)

rosebud@inet.com

CAREER OBJECTIVE: Audit Management.

WORK EXPERIENCE

Jordan Marsh, Ft. Myers, FL
Audit Manager, 1992 - present

Oversee analytical review and verification of financial records. Develop audit programs. Establish guidelines for physical distribution of inventory. Evaluate the adequacy of internal controls and the extent of policy compliance. Recommended several audit plans that were implemented by management.

National Textile Co., Miami, FL
Senior Auditor, 1985 - 1990

Conducted financial and operational audits of domestic and international facilities. Conducted an in-depth study of the manufacturing process. Recommended changes in internal controls. Performed EDP audits. Supervised four staff auditors. Saw that effective controls and policies were maintained.

Held & Perkins, Atlanta, GA
Accountant, 1979 - 1985

Handled certified audits of clients in fields of banking, insurance, and construction. Assisted in analysis, verification, and confirmation. Prepared financial statements, SEC reports, and budget plans.

EDUCATION

University of Kentucky, Louisville, KY
M.B.A. in Finance, 1992

University of Kentucky, Louisville, KY
B.A. in Accounting, 1978

SPECIAL SKILLS

Fluent in Spanish and French. Extensive experience using Microsoft Office, specifically Excel.

REFERENCES PROVIDED UPON REQUEST.

JEFF DAMEN
666 E. Westlake Drive
Dallas, TX 78787
Phone: (214) 555-6629
E-mail: damenj@flowers4u.com

Professional Experience

Internet Project Manager

FLOWERS4U, INC., June '99 - present
Dallas, TX

Managed website development project for florist company: www.flowers4u.com. Consulted principal for site goals, design, and presentation. Managed copywriter, graphic artist, and photographer. Negotiated with Internet service provider and telecom vendors.

Marketing Manager

BASF, INC., January '97 - June '99
Riverside, CA

Managed marketing department consisting of four employees: website business manager, event coordinator, advertising coordinator, and graphic designer. Managed nationwide public relations, marketing, and advertising campaigns to launch new website www.basf.com. Increased sales 22 percent over 18-month period. Prepared advertising strategies and overall advertising plans. Managed the design of brochures, survey results, reports, and sales collateral from concept through development. Media buyer (print, broadcast, and outdoor) for local and national advertising campaigns.

Manager of Information Systems

BASF, INC., May '93 - December '96

System Administrator of corporate LAN with 70 Macintosh and 30 Windows NT computers. Configured and managed company Internet access and E-mail system. Corporate buyer of computer hardware and software. Skilled at negotiating terms. Analyzed and solved LAN software and hardware problems. Assisted account executives with software training and problems. Produced reports for company executives. Customized database for senior management special projects.

Office Manager

HEALY & ASSOCIATES, October '93 - April '93
Palo Alto, CA

Managed central California regional sales office and database. Configured Macintosh computer system and installed LAN, database, and functional software. Assisted regional sales director in developing marketing communications strategy.

Education

SAN FRANCISCO STATE UNIVERSITY, San Francisco, CA, 1992
Bachelor of Arts in Advertising
Minor: Business Administration

Technical Expertise/Computer Skills

Cross-platform experience with Windows and Macintosh networks and applications: ACI
US 4th Dimension Database, Macromedia Dreamweaver, Microsoft Internet Explorer, MS
Office, MS PowerPoint, MS Project, Netscape Communicator.
Desktop publishing: QuarkXPress, Adobe Photoshop.
World Wide Web applications and Hypertext Markup Language (HTML, DHTML).

Awards

Phi Kappa Phi, National Scholastic Honor Society
Kappa Tau Alpha, National Journalism Honor Society

References provided upon request

HARRISON G. BUNWADDIE

55 E. Huron St.
Chicago, IL 60601
708/555-2900 (Day)
708/555-2810 (Evening)
bunwaddie@earthlink.net

WORK EXPERIENCE

Sandler Electronics Inc., Chicago, IL
Industrial Relations Manager, 1993 - present

Oversaw all labor relations between the corporation and the union. Worked with the personnel department to plan labor policy, negotiate contracts, review hiring practices, and maintain records. Participated on grievance committees. Advised Vice President of Personnel on legal matters. Supervised a staff of ten employees.

Good Cereal Co., Battle Creek, MI
Assistant Personnel Manager, 1988 - 1993

Supervised a staff of eight interviewers and testers for hiring of office and warehouse personnel. Assisted Personnel Manager with all department operations. Oversaw all records for warehouse personnel. Developed a successful training and evaluation program for all company employees.

IBM, Chicago, IL
Personnel Intern, 1987 - 1988

Assisted with testing and evaluation of prospective employees. Scheduled interviews. Maintained computer database.

EDUCATION

Northwestern University, Evanston, IL
Juris Doctor, 1988
Admitted to the Michigan Bar Association, 1988

Garrison College, Terre Haute, IN
B.S. in Management, 1984

REFERENCES PROVIDED ON REQUEST.

SANDRA EMILY HARRIS
7700 Lake Shore Drive
Chicago, IL 60606
312/555-4155

OBJECTIVE

A management position in the insurance industry.

WORK EXPERIENCE

Urbina Underwriters, Inc., Chicago, IL
1995 - present

Served as assistant claims representative with a specialty in auto insurance. Promoted to senior claims representative. Handled commercial properties. Managed a staff of seven employees. Interfaced with senior management.

Walker & Associates, Atlanta, GA
1993 - 1995

Hired as junior insurance investigator. Promoted to assistant claims representative. Handled various types of insurance claims.

EDUCATION

Southwest College, College Park, GA
B.S. in Marketing, 1992

Hoffman Estates High School, Chicago, IL
Graduated 1988

REFERENCES

Provided on request.

ANTHONY RUTHERFORD

7900 Mile High Ave.   807-555-4949
Salt Lake City, UT 84126   807-555-2911

GOAL:

Vice President of Operations at a reputable banking institution.

ACHIEVEMENTS:

- Assisted Senior Vice President in day-to-day operations.
- Directed work procedures in light of bank policy.
- Managed assets, securities, and bank records.
- Established all operating procedures and policies in the department.
- Oversaw restructuring of MIS Department.
- Coordinated duties of department personnel.
- Served on bank policy review board.
- Assisted in the planning of branch locations.
- Handled accounting and financial analysis.
- Approved and declined credit for loans.

WORK HISTORY:

FIRST NATIONAL BANK OF UTAH, Salt Lake City, UT
Assistant Vice President, 1988 - present

FIRST NATIONAL BANK OF UTAH, Provo, UT
Branch Director, 1983 - 1988

SANTA FE BANK, Santa Fe, NM
Teller, 1982 - 1983

EDUCATION:

WASHINGTON STATE UNIVERSITY, Tacoma, WA
B.S. in Accounting, 1980

References available on request.

EMMY DANO

1600 Roberts St.
Oakland, CA 92112
415/555-4155
emmy@netcom.net

CAREER OBJECTIVE

A position as an insurance underwriter leading to management.

WORK EXPERIENCE

Peterson Underwriters, Inc., San Francisco, CA
1996 - present

Served as assistant claims representative with a specialty in auto insurance. Promoted to senior claims representative. Handled commercial properties. Managed a staff of seven employees. Interfaced with senior management.

E. Katsulos Associates, Andover, MD
1994 - 1996

Hired as junior insurance investigator. Promoted to assistant claims representative. Handled various types of insurance claims.

EDUCATION

Parker College, Andover, MD
B.S. in Marketing, 1993

Hoffman High School, Oakland, CA
Graduated 1989

REFERENCES

Available upon request.

TYRELL STEVENSON
602 S. Texas Ave.
Oakland, CA 94611
415/555-3168
tyrell22@hotmail.com

EDUCATION:

International School of Business, San Francisco, CA
2/99 - present
Major: Hotel Management

World Travel Institute, Sacramento, CA
1991 - 1992
Certificate, Travel Consultant

Eastern Illinois University, Charleston, IL
Attended 1990 - 1992
Area of concentration: business management

WORK EXPERIENCE:

Reddman, Inc., Oakland, CA
Manager/Salesman, 11/97 - present

Managed own cookware business. Sold cookware at wholesale, retail, and over the Internet. Negotiated prices with customers. Handled all finances and bookkeeping.

Sacramento Jewelry, Sacramento, CA
Manager, 1/96 - 11/97

Managed a retail jewelry store. Oversaw all aspects of sales, purchasing, and bookkeeping. Supervised two employees.

Westerly Travel, Chicago, IL
Travel Consultant, 4/92 - 1/96

Sold airline tickets and tour packages. Advised customers on travel plans. Handled ARC reports to airline corporations.

References available on request.

GINA STEVENSON

433 Maple Drive
Hoffman Estates, IL 60035
708/555-2341

OBJECTIVE

To manage a Laura Ashley store.

WORK EXPERIENCE

Gina Designs, Hoffman Estates, IL

Owner/Designer, 1988 - present
Established a national market for my original clothing line. Displayed and merchandised clothing items at retail stores and fashion shows. Increased sales 300 percent in the past two years. Ordered supplies, processed purchase orders and invoices. Shipped and delivered products.

Talbot's Inc., Schaumburg, IL

Assistant Sales Manager, 1989 - present
Sold clothing and gifts at the retail level. Increased sales by developing in-store promotions. Ordered stock and maintained inventory.

Lynn's Hallmark, Arlington Heights, IL

Manager, 1983 - 1988
Salesperson, 1978 - 1982
Managed gift shop and supervised 10 employees. Maintained inventory, sales records, and bank deposits. Ordered products, processed purchase orders and invoices. Handled all payroll duties. Sold gift items.

EDUCATION

B.A., Interior Design, Wheaton College, Wheaton, IL, 1988

SPECIAL SKILLS

Working knowledge of Spanish.
Experience working with WordPerfect and Microsoft Office 2000.

REFERENCES

Provided on request.

IVAN P. LINS

24 E. Saginaw
Crystal Lake, IL 60203
708/555-3894
lins@globaldance.net

OBJECTIVE

A position as a marketing manager where I can use my knowledge and experience in sales and marketing.

RELEVANT ACCOMPLISHMENTS

- Managed sales of all product lines in midwestern markets for a leading maker of textiles.
- Represented five corporate divisions of the company with sales in excess of $3 million annually.
- Directed and motivated a sales force of 12 sales representatives in planned selling toward specific goals.
- Built wholesale and dealer distribution substantially as District Manager.
- Handled both internal and external sales and marketing for an office supply manufacturer.
- Oversaw all aspects of samples, advertising, and marketing.
- Maintained good customer relations with retail stores.

EMPLOYMENT HISTORY

ROBEAU INDUSTRIES, Chicago, IL
Regional Sales Manager, 1993 - present

CAROLINA CO., Elgin, IL
District Manager, 1988 - 1993

SUPER OFFICE SUPPLY, INC., St. Louis, MO
Assistant to the Sales Manager, 1984 - 1988

EDUCATION

UNIVERSITY OF MICHIGAN, Ann Arbor, MI
B.A. in Business Administration, 1983

Major: Marketing
Minor: Spanish

SEMINARS

National Management Association Seminar, 1992

Chicago University Seminars, 1995 - 1998

PROFESSIONAL MEMBERSHIPS

Sales and Marketing Association of Chicago

National Association of Market Developers

REFERENCES AVAILABLE ON REQUEST.

TERRENCE LEONG
9021 W. Cedar Lane
Grand Rapids, MI 50399
616-555-2002

OBJECTIVE

To become manager of a Thai-Chinese restaurant in the Grand Rapids area.

WORK EXPERIENCE

SHANGHAI RESTAURANT, Grand Rapids, MI

Assistant Manager, 1991 - present

Supervised kitchen, dining, and bar staff of 25. Maintained food and linen stocks. Hired waitstaff and busboys. Approved menus. Assisted in the placement of advertising.

PANCAKE WORLD, St. Louis, MO

Assistant Quality Control Director, 1987 - 1991

Evaluated and maintained performance standards at several restaurants. Oversaw food, service, and cleanliness. Prepared reports and made recommendations for improvements.

CALIFORNIA CAFE, East St. Louis, IL

Assistant Manager, 1985 - 1987

Supervised breakfast service at a busy neighborhood cafe. Hired and evaluated employees. Maintained food stocks. Handled various financial matters.

ROSE'S, Chicago, IL

Cook, 1982 - 1985

Prepared various deli-style meals for a local restaurant.

EDUCATION

WHEATON COLLEGE, Wheaton, IL

Studied for two years, 1980 - 1982

Majored in business

LYONS TOWNSHIP HIGH SCHOOL, La Grange, IL

Graduated, 1978

REFERENCES

Available upon request.

STEVEN TYLER
17001 E. Riverside Dr.
Burbank, CA 91505
818/555-3728 (Day)
818/555-9000 (Night)
styler@pvac.com

RELEVANT ACHIEVEMENTS

Marketing

- Implemented various promotional programs including product, visuals, giveaways, and delivery of presentation.
- Conceived and developed creative product promotions.
- Designed unique advertising with innovative placements, including billboards, trade publications, and newspapers.
- Administered advertising budget.
- Represented company to both industry and media.

Sales

- Exceeded revenue goals by 41 percent this last year.
- Set annual sales records in 1996 with revenues of $55 million.
- Administered a $125 million advertising budget.

Management

- Restructured Paradise Vacations, achieving #1 position in sales for the western U.S.
- Designed and wrote new policy manuals and job descriptions for all departments.
- Trained staff and managers in order to increase productivity.
- Directed the sales force in achieving and exceeding sales goals.
- Oversaw development of Paradise Vacations website.

EMPLOYMENT HISTORY

Paradise Vacations, Burbank, CA
Senior Vice President, 1995 - present
Vice President, Sales and Marketing, 1994 - 1995

Western Airlines, San Diego, CA
Vice President of Sales, 1992 - 1994
Director, Sales Department, 1989 - 1992

SAS Airlines, Los Angeles, CA
Regional Sales Manager, 1984 - 1989
District Sales Manager, 1980 - 1984

TWA, Houston, TX
Sales Representative, 1975 - 1980

United Plastics, Inc., Beverly Glen, CA
Sales Representative, 1968 - 1973

EDUCATION

Colorado University, Denver, CO
M.B.A., 1975
Graduated with honors

Revers College, Beaver Falls, KY
B.S. in Communications, 1967

SEMINARS

International Sales and Marketing
Domestic Sales and Marketing
Management and Administration
Travel Sales Incentives
Telemarketing

REFERENCES

Available on request.

MARYLOU BADEMACHER

1414 N. Montebello Drive
Berkeley, CA 98028
415/555-4930

EDUCATION: University of California at Berkeley
                       Bachelor of Science in Business
                       Expected June 2001

HONORS: Beta Gamma Upsilon Honorary Society
                       Dean's List
                       Manley Writing Award, 1999

ACTIVITIES: Treasurer, Gamma Gamma Gamma Sorority
                       Freshman Advisor
                       Homecoming Planning Committee
                       Alumni Welcoming Committee

WORK EXPERIENCE: AT&T, New York, NY
                       Marketing Intern, 2000

                       Assisted marketing staff in the areas of research, demographics, sales
                       forecasts, identifying new customers, and Internet promotion.

                       University of California at Berkeley
                       Office Assistant, Journalism School, 1998 - 2000

                       Assisted with registrations, filing, and typing. Arranged application
                       materials. Assembled course packs.

SPECIAL SKILLS: Fluent in German. Hands-on computer experience using
                       Microsoft Office 2000.

REFERENCES: Available on request.

BONNIE THORNTON
236 Bainbridge Street
Malden, MA 01245
bonnie2000@aol.com
617/555-2291

WORK EXPERIENCE:

SAMUEL GOMPERS, CO., Boston, MA   1994 - 2000

Finance Director

Plan and execute certified and interim audits of diversified client companies. Prepare time budgets and audit programs. Review and evaluate internal accounting controls. Prepare and analyze financial statements. Supervise and evaluate staff assigned to each audit.

LEWIS, MURROW & CO., Boston, MA   1985 - 1993

Senior Accountant

Joined this firm as Semi-Senior Accountant and advanced to seniority in 1987. Participated in audits of initially smaller client companies and ultimately advanced to auditing responsibilities with larger accounts.

S. J. TILDEN & COMPANY, Boston, MA   1983 - 1985

Accountant

Gained my initial experience in the field of public accounting with this firm.

EDUCATION:

BOSTON COLLEGE, Boston, MA

B.S. in Accounting, 1982
Earned C.P.A. in 1985

AFFILIATIONS:

American Institute of Certified Public Accountants

Massachusetts State Society of Certified Public Accountants

REFERENCES:

Provided upon request.

DIANA SIMPLETON
2323 Canon Drive
Beverly Hills, CA 90120
Telephone: 213/555-8920

ACHIEVEMENTS

Sales/Promotion

- Sold Clinique cosmetic products in two major retail stores.
- Orchestrated product demonstrations to customers in store.
- Designed displays of merchandise.
- Represented Clinique at promotional events in the Los Angeles area advising customers on the use of skin care products.
- Maintained inventory and handled monthly sales reports.
- Developed an advertising campaign that addressed distribution, market share, and sales promotion for a line of women's clothing as a class assignment.

Management

- Managed Clinique counter at The Broadway and at Robinsons-May.
- Supervised three salespeople.
- Gained knowledge of marketing management techniques through classes.

EMPLOYMENT HISTORY

Clinique, The Broadway, Glendale, CA
Counter Manager, 1995 - present

Clinique, Robinsons-May Department Store, Beverly Hills, CA
Retail Salesperson, 1993 - 1995

Geffen Records, Los Angeles, CA
Switchboard Operator, 1992

EDUCATION

B.S. in Business from Santa Clara College, Santa Clara, CA - 1992

THEODORE ATONE

3300 Topper Ave. #44
Burbank, CA 91505
818/555-2909
theoatone@aol.com

JOB OBJECTIVE: CIRCULATION MANAGEMENT.

SKILLS & ACCOMPLISHMENTS:

Developed and implemented all circulation and related programs. Assisted in the areas of advertising and promotion. Devised and coordinated merchandise marketing programs. Oversaw the following areas:

- Subscription promotion.
- Direct response.
- Graphics buying.
- Fulfillment.
- Budgets.
- Agency sales.
- Newsstand sales.
- On-line sales.

WORK HISTORY:

Sea Publishing Co., Los Angeles, CA
Circulation Director, 1996 - present

On Magazine, Los Angeles, CA
Circulation Director, 1991 - 1996

Phoenix Magazine, Phoenix, AZ
Assistant Circulation Director, 1988 - 1991

Briis Publishing, New York, NY
Assistant Operations Manager, 1984 - 1987

EDUCATION:

Southwest College, Phoenix, AZ
B.A. in English, 1983

Phoenix School of Business Administration,
Phoenix, AZ, 1984

REFERENCES PROVIDED UPON REQUEST.

PETER THOMASSON

Fulton Hall

2300 East Harrison

Room 306

Chicago, IL 60633

312/555-4849

bullsfan@mci.net

OBJECTIVE:

A career in the field of finance.

EDUCATION:

University of Illinois at Chicago, Chicago, IL
Bachelor of Arts in Economics
Expected June 2000

HONORS:

Phi Beta Kappa
Dean's List five times
Robeson Business Scholarship, 1998

ACTIVITIES:

Vice President, Beta Gamma Fraternity
Freshman Advisor
Homecoming Planning Committee
Baseball Team
Student Rights Group

WORK EXPERIENCE:

IBM, Northbrook, IL
Accounting Intern, 1999

Assisted finance department in the areas of accounting, bookkeeping, financial statements, forecasts, and planning. Extensively used spreadsheet software programs.

University of Illinois at Chicago
Office Assistant, Journalism School, 1997 - 1999

Assisted with registrations, filing, and typing. Arranged application materials. Assembled course packs.

General Office, Registrar, 1997

Processed transcript requests. Entered registrations on the computer. Provided informational assistance to students.

SPECIAL SKILLS:

Hands-on computer experience using Microsoft Office.

REFERENCES:

Available on request.

PEDRO RENFRO
111 E. 4th St.
Rockford, IL 68899
815/555-2931

CAREER OBJECTIVE

Assistant Manager of the Accounting Division of large corporation with the goal of promotion to Manager.

WORK EXPERIENCE

MARSHALL FIELD'S, Rockford, IL

Accounts Payable Supervisor, 1994 - present

Handle both yearly and quarterly accruals and reconciliations. Supervise seven people. Oversee up to 50 vendor adjustments and inquiries per day. Monitor expenses. Process and route checks.

JONES, INC., Des Moines, IA

Accounts Payable Manager, 1989 - 1994

Oversaw all department activities. Processed several hundred invoices per day. Audited vendor invoices for payment. Supervised 20 people. Handled vendor inquiries and adjustments.

HART'S DETERGENT, INC., Hillsboro, SD

Assistant Manager, Accounts Payable, 1981 - 1988

Processed 400 - 500 invoices per day. Supervised 10 people. Oversaw bookkeeping, check requests, and disbursements.

HANDLEMAN & HANDLEMAN, Fort Dix, SC

Billing Coordinator, 1977 - 1981

Billed invoices. Handled accounts receivable and accounts payable.

EDUCATION

HANOVER HIGH SCHOOL, Fort Dix, SC

Earned diploma, 1976
Concentration in mathematics

REFERENCES PROVIDED ON REQUEST.

RANDALL BERTRAND KENNEDY
7901 Martella Ave.
New Orleans, LA 29920
504/555-2900 (Day)
504/555-2810 (Evening)
rbk@earthlink.net

WORK EXPERIENCE

Johannson, Inc., New Orleans, LA

Industrial Relations Manager, 1994 - present

Oversaw all labor relations between the corporation and the union. Worked with the personnel department to plan labor policy, negotiate contracts, review hiring practices, and maintain records. Participated on grievance committees. Advised Vice President of Personnel on legal matters. Supervised a staff of ten employees.

Target Discount Stores, Inc., Los Angeles, CA

Assistant Personnel Manager, 1989 - 1994

Supervised a staff of eight interviewers and testers for hiring of office and warehouse personnel. Assisted Personnel Manager with all department operations. Oversaw all records for warehouse personnel. Developed a successful training and evaluation program for all company employees.

Republic Telephone, Inc., Detroit, MI

Personnel Intern, 1988 - 1989

Assisted with testing and evaluation of prospective employees. Scheduled interviews. Maintained records.

EDUCATION

University of Michigan, Ann Arbor, MI

Juris Doctor, 1989
Admitted to the Michigan Bar Association, 1989

University of Virginia, Norfolk, VA

B.S. in Management, 1985

REFERENCES

Available on request

ROBERT HAMMOND

16119 Sea View Drive

La Jolla, CA 91201

619/555-2221

robhamm@pacbell.net

WORK EXPERIENCE

La Jolla Motel, La Jolla, CA

Manager, 1996 - present
Handled all bookkeeping, payroll, personnel, advertising, and public relations. Developed a successful advertising campaign that increased convention business 33 percent. Oversaw the implementation of an expansion program.

Assistant Manager, 1993 - 1996
Managed front office, switchboard, groundskeepers, and housekeepers. Hired and trained all personnel. Handled all purchasing and payroll activities. Directed convention and banquet facilities.

Desk Clerk, 1992 - 1993
Handled all registration, reservations, and billing. Informed housekeeping of arrivals and departures of guests. Issued keys and distributed mail.

EDUCATION

San Jose High School, San Jose, CA

Graduated 1991

REFERENCES

Available on request

JEFFERY P. STOUT

14-44 E. Tyrone Ave.
Omaha, NE 49940
402/555-3210

OBJECTIVE: Business Management

EDUCATION

University of Nebraska, Omaha, NE
M.B.A. expected June 2000
Area of Concentration: Financial Management/Accounting Management

Shreveport College, Shreveport, LA
B.A. 1997
Major: Economics
Minor: Political Science

WORK EXPERIENCE

University of Nebraska, Omaha, NE
Analytical Studies Intern, 1998 - present
Collected and organized data for a university finance study.
Conducted library research. Edited draft of final report.

Shreveport College, Shreveport, LA
Resident Hall Assistant, 1995 - 1997
Oversaw all aspects of a college dormitory. Supervised residents, kitchen
and maintenance staff. Served as a liaison to the Student Affairs Office.

OTHER JOBS

Waiter, Limousine Driver, House Painter

References available as requested.

DAVID CHANG

677 Rosewood Drive
San Jose, CA 99002
510-555-9090
dchang@webnet.com
www.davidchang.com

Goal: A position in business management and development for an Internet start-up.

Education:

June 1998: Master of Business Administration - Florida State University, Jacksonville, FL
June 1994: Bachelor of Arts: Computer Science - University of California, Northridge, CA

Experience:

1998 - Present: Kmart - Operations Analyst & Distribution Management
Analyze regional distribution center operations and best methods.
Manage external seasonal distribution center.
Supervise and work with team members from various departments.
Prepare and analyze forecasts, budgets, and internal reports.
Control production by managing volume inflow and outflow.
Identify opportunities for more efficient and safer product movement.
Manage the building budget and monitor warehouse expenditures.
Provide the center with staffing models to ensure optimal staffing levels.
Assist in recruiting efforts through job fairs, building tours, and interviews.

1995 - Present: MacServ - Business Partner, Consultant, Developer, & Technician
Provide computer consultation to homes, businesses, and schools.
Provide regular maintenance and troubleshooting of computer systems.
Provide training in major software programs for Macintosh and Windows.
Develop FileMaker Pro applications for businesses.

1994 - 1998: Computer Warehouse - Retail Management, Market Analyst, & Computer Instructor
Oversaw sales and marketing of all products and services.
Analyzed market competitiveness and evaluated product performance.
Communicated and coordinated vendor marketing events and programs.
Provided customer assistance and resolution of customer complaints.
Supervised, scheduled, trained, and reviewed up to 60 employees.
Maintained inventory through store audits and security checks.
Trained corporations in the operation of computer hardware and software.
Administered, maintained, and troubleshot store computer network.

References available on request.

HANNAH P. WEAVER
14 E. Main St.
Dubuque, IA 33333
319/555-8375
hpw2@aol.com

CAREER OBJECTIVE: Manager of a general bookstore.

WORK EXPERIENCE

Templeman Books, Dubuque, IA

Manager, 1995 - present

Managed all aspects of a retail bookstore. Oversaw maintenance and selection of inventory. Supervised four employees. Increased sales 20 percent in first three years. Coordinated design and development of store website.

Templeman Books, Dubuque, IA

Management Trainee, 1994 - 1995

Learned all aspects of retail bookselling. Sold books, handled customer relations, made sales presentations, designed displays.

Dubuque Camera Shop, Dubuque, IA

Salesperson, 1992 - 1994

Sold cameras. Processed film orders. Repaired cameras. Assisted customers with their photographic needs.

EDUCATION

Dubuque College, Dubuque, IA

B.A. in Literature, 1992

Graduated with honors

Student Council

Ski Club

PROFESSIONAL MEMBERSHIPS

National Association of Booksellers
Dubuque Business League

REFERENCES

Provided upon request.

CARMEN McRAE

7 E. Magnolia

Atlanta, GA 24990

Phone: 404/555-7449

ACCOMPLISHMENTS

- Managed administrative activities of a staff of 250.
- Designed improved administrative, clerical, and payroll systems, which resulted in significant savings.
- Oversaw operational studies of the activities and organizational structure of client companies.
- Introduced new purchasing, shipping, and billing procedures.
- Received a high percentage of acceptance on recommendations to upper management.
- Conducted a study of clerical operations in the purchasing department and attained a 20 percent reduction in department budget.
- Revised printing operations, which increased cost efficiency.
- Oversaw the installation of a computer network for the department.

EMPLOYMENT HISTORY

1990 - present	NUMARK SYSTEMS, INC., Atlanta, GA *Administrative Manager*
1985 - 1990	PARKER LEWIS, INC., New York, NY *Accounting Consultant*
1979 - 1985	AMERICAN NATIONAL CORP., White Plains, NY *Systems Analyst*
1976 - 1979	SANDERSON CO., New York, NY *Assistant Systems Analyst*
1973 - 1976	AT&T, Chicago, IL *Accountant*

Page 1 of 2

EDUCATION

UNIVERSITY OF GEORGIA, Atlanta, GA
M.B.A., 1972
B.A. in Economics, 1970

REFERENCES

Available upon request.

BRIDGETT TERRY

4444 24th St.

Los Angeles, CA 91809

213/555-3411

bridgettt@netzero.com

OBJECTIVE: A management position in personnel administration.

WORK EXPERIENCE:

WOODBINE & CO., Los Angeles, CA

Payroll Specialist, 1992 - present

Determine job grading system. Evaluate jobs. Maintain employee budget. Conduct performance appraisals. Decide wage increases and adjustments. Set salary ranges. Write job descriptions. Coordinate compensation surveys. Gather data on vacations, sick time, and leaves of absence.

EDUCATION:

UNIVERSITY OF CALIFORNIA AT BERKELEY

Bachelor's Degree in Economics, 1991

PERSONNEL MANAGEMENT INSTITUTE

Lorminon College, Dallas, TX
Summer 1997

HONORS:

UCSB Economics Scholarship, 1989 - 1990
Elected Student Government Secretary, 1990
Gamma Kappa Phi Honorary Society, 1990 - 1991

REFERENCES:

Available upon request.

PATRICK H. McCOY
1701 N. Hampshire Pl.
Miami, FL 33126
305/555-3909
305/555-9099

OBJECTIVE

A management position for a furnace manufacturer.

WORK EXPERIENCE

NEWMARK FURNACE CO., Miami, FL
Account Executive, 1995 - present

Handled accounts for southern Florida area. Expanded customer base by 28 percent during my tenure. Conducted field visits to solve customer complaints. Maintained daily contact with customers to ensure good company/customer relations. Wrote product information flyers and distributed them to potential customers.

POTISCO, Terre Haute, IN
Sales Representative, 1991 - 1995

Sold to customers, particularly contractors. Priced bid estimates as required. Oversaw customer and public relations, which helped to build company's image. Set up office procedures where necessary.

HONOCO, INC., Chicago, IL
Sales Representative, 1988 - 1991

Developed and managed new territories. Built sales through calls on physicians, hospitals, retailers, and wholesalers. Developed creative techniques for increasing product sales. Maintained current knowledge of competitive products.

EDUCATION

WHEATON COLLEGE, Wheaton, IL
B.S. in Business, 1987

SEMINARS

Sales and Marketing for the 90s
Florida Business Association
Marketing for the Furnace Industry

REFERENCES

Available upon request.

Zoe Terre

839 Wilton St.

Pittsburgh, PA 15100

412/555-2902

terre1@aol.com

OBJECTIVE

Management position in a medium- to large-sized accounting firm.

SKILLS & CAPABILITIES

- Maintained ledgers.
- Prepared invoices and vouchers.
- Supplied periodic financial statements.
- Assisted with internal auditing.
- Handled accounts payable and receivable.
- Directed a bookkeeping staff of ten employees.
- Experienced with most accounting software.

EMPLOYMENT HISTORY

American Marine Co., Pittsburgh, PA
Accounts Manager, 1990 - present

Parker College, Philadelphia, PA
Assistant Finance Manager, 1987 - 1990

Brentwood & Associates, Philadelphia, PA
Billing Supervisor, 1985 - 1987

NBC, Inc., New York, NY
Bookkeeper, 1984 - 1985

EDUCATION

Peters Junior College, Santa Fe, NM
Business Certificate, 1984

REFERENCES

Available on request.

JOEL JAMES III
1441 S. Goebert
Providence, RI 00231
401/555-1234
401/555-3782

Objective

President of a publishing corporation where I can apply my management, promotion, and marketing experience.

Employment History

JOHNSON PUBLISHING CORPORATION, Providence, RI

Vice President, Advertising, 1988 - present

Promoted from Marketing Manager to Vice President of Advertising after three years. Managed all phases of publishing properties including

> *Furniture Magazine*
>
> *Home Improvement Weekly*
>
> *Scuba Digest*
>
> *Travel Age Magazine*
>
> *Pharmacy News*

Established and developed the first newspaper advertising mat service in the furniture industry. Increased distributors and retailers using this service by 55 percent in three years. Improved the effectiveness and volume of all retail advertising.

REBUS PUBLISHING COMPANY, Boston, MA

Advertising Manager, 1979 - 1987

Serviced and developed accounts throughout the eastern United States. Handled advertising for publications in the restaurant industry. Increased sales in my territories every year by at least 21 percent.

TIME MAGAZINE, New York, NY

Assistant Advertising Promotion Manager, 1975 - 1979

Spearheaded original promotion program that increased revenue 33 percent in two years. Developed new markets. Helped to improve company/customer relations.

ROYAL CROWN COLA CORPORATION, Chicago, IL

Division Sales Manager, 1972 - 1975

Promoted from salesman to sales manager after one year. Organized sampling campaigns and in-store and restaurant displays. Directed bottlers' cooperative advertising and point-of-purchase displays.

Education

DRAKE UNIVERSITY, Des Moines, IA

B.A. in Economics, 1971
Graduated Phi Beta Kappa
Top 5 percent of class

Professional Affiliations

ROCKING CHAIR, social and professional organization of the furniture industry, President, 1996 - 1998

BEVERAGE ASSOCIATION of AMERICA
Board of Directors

PUBLISHERS ASSOCIATION
Advisory Committee

References

Available upon request.

Gerald Holsten

1205 Maple Avenue
Elsmere, Delaware 19807
Tel. 302-456-7112
E-mail: superG@netcomm.net

Objective: Management position in personnel training and development.

Experience:

Administration and Development

Developed intra-school program to improve staff morale and instruction. Created a special program for incoming high school students to facilitate their adjustment to a new environment. Administered a remediation and orientation program for newly admitted students to high school. Developed and supervised the operations of a college counseling office designed to service 2000 high school students. Planned career and college fair programs for students. Acted as school liaison to college admissions and financial aid offices and personnel. Published college and career newsletters.

Placement Counseling

Counseled unemployed clients in a training program for the purpose of job placement. Provided supportive counseling services to clients while they trained for employment. Vocational, career, college, and financial aid counseling and placement for population seeking post-secondary education and training. Individual and group counseling and large group presentations.

Teaching and Training

Conducted sessions to improve client's communications and job interviewing skills. Trained professional and volunteer staff in college admissions and financial aid counseling. Supervised student teachers in their training. Taught and developed curricula in psychology, sociology, and basic learning skills.

Employment History:

1989 – Present	Abraham Lincoln High School
1996 (Summer Employment)	GE Employment and Training Systems
1989 – 1993	Thomas Jefferson High School

Education:

B.A. (History), 1980 - University of Wisconsin
M.S. (Counseling), 1988 - University of Wisconsin
Advanced Certificate (Counseling), 1989 - University of Wisconsin

Affiliations:

American Personnel and Guidance Association
American Psychological Association
Association of Teachers of Social Studies

MARLENE MAREGO
55 E. Wood St.
White Plains, NY 10604
914/555-1234
914/555-2938

WORK EXPERIENCE

ITC, INC., WHITE PLAINS, NY

Executive Vice President, Special Projects, 1991 - present

Managed all administrative operations. Directed the work of several project units simultaneously. Created and implemented organizational policy. Planned and developed programs and publications. Designed promotional materials. Oversaw website development.

AMERICAN DEVELOPMENT, INC., MIAMI, FL

Director of Operations, 1984 - 1991

Managed all educational and personnel projects. Prepared proposals for public and private funding. Assisted in technical management functions. Evaluated operations to ensure effective implementation of contractual requirements. Negotiated contracts.

CERTA CORPORATION, JACKSON, MS

Account Executive, 1980 - 1984

Handled accounts for all of Mississippi. Expanded customer base by 30 percent during tenure. Conducted field visits to solve customer complaints. Maintained daily contact with customers to ensure good company/customer relations. Wrote product information flyers and distributed them to potential customers.

EDUCATION

NEW YORK UNIVERSITY, NEW YORK, NY

M.B.A. with Honors, 1980

UNIVERSITY OF MISSISSIPPI, JACKSON, MS

B.A. in Economics, 1978

MEMBERSHIPS

New York Association of Business Executives

National Business Association

REFERENCES

Provided upon request.

GINA CAROL STONE

5001 Lincoln Drive #2
Marlton, NJ 08053
609/555-1200
609/555-3893
gcs@inet.com

OBJECTIVE

Sales manager of a paper products company.

PROFESSIONAL EXPERIENCE

Harrison Paper Co., Philadelphia, PA
District Sales Manager, 1992 - 1998

Planned successful strategies to identify and develop new accounts. Increased sales by at least 20 percent each year (50 percent in 1996). Researched and analyzed market conditions to seek out new customers. Developed weekly and monthly sales strategies. Supervised seven sales representatives.

Daniel P. Miller & Co., Trenton, NJ
Sales Representative, 1985 - 1992

Developed and managed new territories. Built sales through calls on retailers and wholesalers. Developed creative techniques for increasing product sales. Maintained current knowledge of competitive products. Wrote weekly and monthly sales reports.

Sammy's Best Burger Co., Newark, NJ
Assistant to Sales Manager, 1978 - 1985

Handled both internal and external sales and marketing, including samples, advertising, and pricing. Served as company sales representative and sold a variety of products to retail stores.

EDUCATION

New Jersey State University, Trenton, NJ
B.A. in Botany, 1977
Graduated in top 10 percent of class
Recipient of Floyd T. Harper Botany Scholarship

SPECIAL SKILLS

Programming experience in Virtual Basic. Software programs used: Lotus, WordPerfect. Working knowledge of Russian.

REFERENCES

Available on request.

JONATHAN P. KILPATRICK
1400 Mercy Court Drive
Sacramento, CA 95590
916/555-3892 (Home)
916/555-9000 (Work)
jonkil22@interland.net

OBJECTIVE: Hospital Administrator for a medium- to large-sized hospital.

SKILLS AND ACHIEVEMENTS

- Planned and implemented procedures and policies for several medical facilities.
- Interviewed and hired administrative staffs.
- Oversaw complex activities in operations and finance.
- Prepared and maintained capital project status and budget reports for various hospitals.
- Oversaw the development of an employee training program.
- Wrote an employee manual.
- Managed commercial medical administration for headquarters as well as divisions.
- Interacted and communicated with the Board of Directors.
- Researched and wrote budget reports and proposals.

EMPLOYMENT HISTORY

Cedar Hospital, Sacramento, CA
Maintenance Control Planner, 1992 - present

Pacific Care Medical Group, San Francisco, CA
Administrative Coordinator, 1988 - 1992

Denver Hospital Collective, Inc., Denver, CO
Director of Planning, 1986 - 1988
Assistant Director of Planning, 1983 - 1986

Englewood Hospital, Englewood, CO
Assistant Administrative Coordinator, 1981 - 1983

page 1 of 2

EDUCATION

University of Colorado, Boulder, CO
Master's in Business Administration, 1981
Graduated Summa Cum Laude

Richmond College, Richmond, CA
Bachelor of Arts in English, 1979

PROFESSIONAL MEMBERSHIPS

California Hospital Association

National Healthcare Administrators Alliance

Sacramento Business Association

REFERENCES

Provided upon request.

PATRICK T. KORAN

39392 Broad Street
Meridian, MS 39301
601-555-2929
ptk@netflash.com
www.patkoran.com

OBJECTIVE:

To work for an established Internet company in business management.

EDUCATION:

Master of Business Administration, 1996

Kellogg School of Business, Northwestern University, Evanston, IL

Emphases: International Marketing and Business, Contract Negotiations

Bachelor of Arts - English, 1992

Northwestern University, Evanston, IL

Minor: Business Administration

EXPERIENCE:

Sole Proprietor - eLand, '98 Dec - Present

Manage own Internet business. Handle Internet Sales, Website Development, and Hosting and Digital Imaging.

Independent Business Consultant, '95 May - '97 May

Ford Group, Syracuse, NY - Software Marketing, Research, Channel Development

Sam's Travel, Baton Rouge, LA - Digital Imaging, Desktop Publishing

Hoge Construction Co., Harrisburg, PA - Job Costing, Strategic Analysis

Fortune's Cookie, Madison, WI - Music Management, Web Page Design, Maintenance

Unistat, Inc., Madison, WI - Market Development, Value-Chain Analysis

Bleecker's, Inc., Chicago, IL - Market Survey, Analysis, Strategic Proposal

Marketing Intern, '92 May - '92 Aug

Alpha Systems, Chicago, IL - Revamped subsidiary reporting method, researched market potential, reviewed congressional activity.

COMPUTER SKILLS:

Adobe Photoshop 5, Dreamweaver 2 (website editor), Microsoft Office 97, Ulead Photoshop 3.0, CorelDRAW, Publisher, WordPerfect Suite, QuattroPro, PageMaker 6.5, Paint Shop Pro, Harvard, DOS 6.22, Win 3.11, Win 95, Win 98, WWW, Navigator, Explorer, Free Agent, SalesLogix (relational sales database), Quicken 2000, Zip, CuteFTP to Linux host site, PC-Tools, dBASE IV, Lotus, Eudora 4, Kodak DC260.

REFERENCES AVAILABLE UPON REQUEST.

CRYSTAL CARTIER

1201 E. Maple Drive

Las Vegas, NV 89901

702/555-9346

Career Objective

An accounting career leading to management.

Skills/Achievements

- Managed insurance, financial, and brokerage accounting.
- Handled general cost accounting procedures.
- Designed systems for budget and cash flow accounting.
- Oversaw contracts, orders, and vouchers.
- Recorded disbursements, tax payments, and expenses.
- Prepared balance sheets.

Work History

HERVEY & CO., Las Vegas, NV

Accountant, 1997 - present

Education

UNIVERSITY OF NEVADA, Las Vegas, NV

B.A. in Accounting, 1996

C.P.A., 1997

References

Provided upon request.

RAMON PARK

16 Port St.
Providence, RI 00727
401/555-9020

CAREER OBJECTIVE:

Credit Manager.

SKILLS & ACCOMPLISHMENTS:

- Conducted studies of clients' financial statements and past credit records.
- Established credit and collection systems.
- Worked with the sales force to develop credit policies.
- Oversaw all credit requests.
- Supervised and reduced delinquent accounts.
- Interviewed applicants for credit and gathered the necessary information for granting credit.
- Simplified credit processing system.
- Maintained good customer relations.
- Reduced turnover in personnel.

EMPLOYMENT HISTORY:

1992 - present	Haring & Andrews, Inc., Providence, RI
	Credit Manager
1988 - 1992	National Credit, Inc., Boston, MA
	Assistant Collections Manager
1986 - 1988	Marshall Field's, Chicago, IL
	Credit Assistant

EDUCATION:

1986	University of Colorado, Boulder, CO
	B.A. in Accounting
	Summa Cum Laude, Dean's List
1990	Providence College, Providence, RI
	Financial Analysis Seminar
1998	Providence College, Providence, RI
	Financial Management Training

IVAR T. KOPESKI

501 W. Glendale Blvd.

Kansas City, MO 51132

816/555-3524

816/555-9090

kop2000@hotmail.com

OBJECTIVE

Regional sales manager for a national manufacturer/distributor

EXPERIENCE

REB Pharmaceuticals, Kansas City, MO

District Sales Manager, 1992 - present

Directed the selling and servicing of accounts to physicians, pharmacies, and hospitals in the Kansas City area. Increased sales by 50 percent in three years. Initiated an incentive plan that resulted in 21 new accounts. Worked with production department to improve product quality.

Jacobs & Jacobs Advertising, Trenton, NJ

Display Coordinator, 1989 - 1992

Coordinated and supervised the installation of displays in men's clothing stores in the Trenton area. Managed a five-person office in all aspects of display planning and production. Worked to help place the firm in the syndicated display advertising field.

Mark Shale, Inc., Schaumburg, IL

Retail Store Manager, 1985 - 1989

Promoted from salesperson to assistant manager to manager within two years. Supervised the designing of display for interior and windows. Handled all aspects of personnel, sales promotions, inventory control, and new products. Interacted with corporate management frequently.

EDUCATION

Harper College, Palatine, IL

Attended two years (1983 - 1985) and majored in advertising.

American Institute, Putnum, NJ

Completed course on sales and marketing techniques, 1991

MEMBERSHIPS

American Display Advertisers

Kansas City Sales Association

Kansas City Community Development Association

REFERENCES

Available on request

RANDALL COURY
62 Collins Place
#43
New Orleans, LA 33290
504/555-3490
504/555-3999

OBJECTIVE

A position as manager of a record store.

EMPLOYMENT HISTORY

WEST RECORDS, NEW ORLEANS, LA

Assistant Manager, 1997 - present

Sold records, waited on customers, assisted in product selection and ordering, handled special orders and returned merchandise. Designed window displays. Oversaw the placement of ads for a major advertising campaign. Represented the store at conventions. Implemented and maintained store website (www .westrecords.com) and E-mail database.

THE BELT STORE, WEST LAKE, LA

Salesperson, 1995 - 1996

Sold accessories to customers, filled special orders, organized and arranged inventory. Handled customer returns and special requests. Assisted in the design of window displays.

EDUCATION

EAST CENTRAL HIGH SCHOOL, New Orleans, LA

Graduated June 1996
Ranked 12th in a class of 200
Tennis Team
Homecoming Committee

REFERENCES

Available on request.

WOODROW ARTHUR TONEY

76 N. Washington Blvd.
Houston, TX 72009
714/555-4890

OBJECTIVE:

A management trainee position in the manufacturing industry.

WORK EXPERIENCE:

R&G Sugar, Inc., Houston, TX

Salesman, 1995 - 1999
Sold refined sugar products to retail businesses. Named top salesman of 1996. Maintained good customer relations by identifying customer needs. Trained new sales representatives and advised them on effective selling techniques.

Popson Camera Co., Milwaukee, WI

Salesman, 1990 - 1995
Sold cameras to retail outfits in the south suburban Milwaukee area. Increased territory sales by 85 percent in five years. Demonstrated and planned specific uses for products in various offices. Maintained constant contact with accounts.

EDUCATION:

Popson Sales Training Course, Milwaukee, WI

Summer 1990

Cobert Technical High School, West Allis, WI

Graduated 1989

Football Team, Cocaptain

REFERENCES:

Available upon request.

MARK T. CHRISTENSON
65 W. Harrison
Minneapolis, MN 44490
612/555-1212 (Day)
612/555-2901 (Night)
marktc@earthlink.net

JOB OBJECTIVE: Regional Manager for a computer software company.

PROFESSIONAL EXPERIENCE

Sales and Promotion

- Made cold calls and visits to software retailers, which resulted in increased accounts.
- Visited and serviced existing accounts to encourage continued sales.
- Advised customers on options available to meet a wide range of product needs.
- Handled dealer requests for information and sample products.
- Oversaw company's E-commerce.

Marketing

- Researched competitive products to evaluate competitors' strengths and weaknesses.
- Planned a marketing strategy that resulted in a significant increase in accounts.
- Maintained demographic data to ascertain buyer profile.

EMPLOYMENT HISTORY

Thomas Software Inc., Minneapolis, MN
Assistant Manager, 1993 - present
Sales Representative, 1991 - 1993

Quaker & Co., St. Paul, MN
Marketing Assistant, 1990

USA Computer Supplies, Skokie, IL
Salesperson, 1988 - 1990

Bennigan's Restaurant, Columbus, OH
Waiter, 1987 - 1988

Page 1 of 2

EDUCATION

Washington University, St. Louis, MO
            B.A. in Business, 1990

HONORS

Phi Beta Kappa, 1990
Honor Roll, 1988 - 1990
Terrance C. Maples Business Scholarship Recipient, 1988, 1989
President, Student Activities Board, 1990

SPECIAL SKILLS

Experience using a variety of word processing, database, and spreadsheet software for both PC and Mac.

REFERENCES

Provided on request.

WILLIAM GAVIN

2666 Western Ave. #44
Madison, WI 55590
414/555-2029

Education:

UNIVERSITY OF WISCONSIN, Madison, WI

M.B.A., 1999

Area of Concentration: Accounting

UNIVERSITY OF CHICAGO, Chicago, IL

B.A. in History, 1996, graduated Summa Cum Laude

Gamma Summa Honorary Society

Leopold Scholarship

Areas of Study:

Basic, intermediate, and advanced accounting

Business law

Cost accounting

Statistical methods

Planning and control

Tax law

Investments

Work History:

WISCONSIN FEDERAL, Madison, WI

Payroll Teller, 1996 - present

Handle transactions with payroll personnel of various companies and organizations involving the distribution of employee checks.

MARSHALL FIELD'S & CO., Chicago, IL

Salesperson, 1994 - 1995

Sold men's clothing at the retail level.

References available

DEREK STRONG

1501 N. Polk Ave.
Springfield, IL 66660
217-555-5552

POSITION DESIRED:

Financial Management Director.

SKILLS & ACHIEVEMENTS:

Research

- Conducted consumer surveys.
- Coordinated policy formulation.
- Developed advertising concepts and strategies.
- Controlled transportation and distribution costs.

Development

- Handled costs forecasting and pricing policies.
- Implemented costing techniques.
- Oversaw research and development budgeting.
- Conducted feasibility studies.

Planning

- Handled long- and short-range financial forecasting.
- Managed capital investment opportunities.
- Made financial projections.
- Directed tax reductions and budgets.

Analysis

- Involved in statistical methodologies and analysis.
- Administered trend analysis.
- Conducted media evaluations and survey designs.

WORK EXPERIENCE:

Control Data, Inc., Springfield, IL
   Senior Financial Analyst, 1988 - present

Warner Co., Jackson, MS
   Financial Analyst, 1978 - 1988

EDUCATION:

Howard University, Washington, DC
   M.A. in Financial Planning, 1978

Thelonious College, Jackson, MS
   B.A. in Economics, 1976

References available on request.

TAWANA SANDRA GOLDMAN
4553 N. Alamo Avenue
Dallas, TX 74667
216/555-8908

OBJECTIVE:

Financial manager for a travel company.

EXPERIENCE:

American Airlines, Inc., Dallas, TX
Customer Service Coordinator, 1995 - present

Sold reservations for domestic flights, hotels, and car rentals. Marketed travel packages through travel agencies. Negotiated airline and hotel discounts for customers. Devised itineraries and solved customers' travel-related problems.

Salt Lake Travel, Salt Lake City, UT
Travel Agent, 1987 - 1995

Handled customer reservations for airlines, hotels, and car rentals. Advised customers on competitive travel packages and prices. Interacted with all major airlines, hotel chains, and car rental companies.

EDUCATION:

University of Illinois, Urbana, IL
B.A. in Business, 1987

SPECIAL SKILLS:

Hands-on experience using most travel-related computer systems, including Sabre. Working knowledge of German, French, and Polish.

REFERENCES:

Available on request.

PAULA STEVENSON
2782 W. 57th St.
Washington, DC 02390
202/555-8908
202/555-7200

OBJECTIVE:

A management position in the import business.

WORK EXPERIENCE:

Sandler Imports, Washington, DC

Manager of Operations, 1994 - present

Managed ten field representatives. Handled information dissemination and distribution. Codesigned a full-color catalog. Placed advertising in major trade publications. Promoted products at trade shows and on company website. Maintained inventory status reports and personnel records.

HTO Publishing Co., Owings Mills, MD

Distribution Assistant, 1987 - 1994

Developed new distribution outlets through cold calls and follow-up visits. Increased distribution in my district by 45 percent over a three-year period. Coordinated a direct-mail program that increased magazine subscriptions 120 percent.

Eastman Kodak Co., Atlanta, GA

Sales Representative, 1982 - 1987

Sold and serviced office copiers to businesses and schools in the greater Atlanta area. Maintained good customer relations through frequent calls and visits. Identified potential customers.

EDUCATION:

Georgetown University, Washington, DC

B.S. in Communications, 1981

PROFESSIONAL MEMBERSHIPS:

National Association of Importers

DC Community Association

Lion's Club

REFERENCES:

Available on request.

THOMAS GEORGE UHR

4220 Woodridge Drive
Ft. Lauderdale, FL 30898
305/555-2898 (Home)
305/555-2900 (Work)
thuhr@aol.com

OBJECTIVE

A career in business management in the technical industry.

SKILLS & ACHIEVEMENTS

MANAGEMENT

- Hired consultant engineers and trained them in technical and interpersonal communications.
- Oversaw the expansion of the department.
- Developed a career path strategy with management, which was successfully implemented.

ADMINISTRATION

- Supervised seven employees responsible for running the central communications operation.
- Handled the inventory of the product development department.
- Wrote and developed a proposal that led to the implementation of a streamlined communications system.

PERSONNEL

- Trained over 300 people, including vice presidents, managers, salespeople, and field engineers.
- Developed course objectives and a task analysis for trainees.
- Oversaw personnel evaluations and made appropriate recommendations.

EMPLOYMENT HISTORY

PORTER & HAWKINS, INC., MIAMI, FL

General Manager, Communications Department, 1994 - present
Assistant Director of Personnel, 1990 - 1994
Technical Instructor, 1987 - 1990
Technician, 1982 - 1987

EDUCATION

UNIVERSITY OF FLORIDA, MIAMI, FL

B.A. in Management, Evening Division, 1989

MIAMI-DADE COMMUNITY COLLEGE, MIAMI, FL

Certificate in Electronics, 1981

REFERENCES

Available upon request.

GEORGE COSTANZA
1711 N. Gurman Ave.
Atlantic City, NJ 02110
609/555-8971

CAREER OBJECTIVE: Restaurant Management.

EXPERIENCE:

Food Service

- Supervised kitchen staff of eight.
- Conducted business with a local catering service.
- Interviewed, hired, and trained student food service workers.
- Catered banquets.
- Served dining patrons as a waiter.

Management

- Ordered and maintained inventory of all food and beverages for a college cafeteria.
- Planned budget and strictly adhered to it.
- Organized work schedules for student workers.
- Managed computerized purchasing, bookkeeping, and payroll.

Food Preparation

- Assisted in the preparation of meals for 90 children and adults at a summer camp.
- Planned meals for 250 resident students.

EMPLOYMENT HISTORY:

Szabo Food Service/Jersey College, Atlantic City, NJ
Food Service Director, 1998 - present

Jersey College, Atlantic City, NJ
Assistant Cafeteria Director, 1997 - 1998

North Shore Children's Camp, Skokie, IL
Dining Hall Director, 1996 - 1997

Paco's Restaurant, Atlantic City, NJ
Waiter, 1995

Tacky's, Garden City, NJ
Busboy, 1994

EDUCATION:

Jersey College, Atlantic City, NJ
B.S. in Business, June 1998

REFERENCES FURNISHED ON REQUEST.

HAROLD C. JONES
Bobb Hall
6 W. Allis Drive
Room 34
Pittsburgh, PA 28920
404/555-2384
bearcub@hotmail.com

OBJECTIVE:

Position in sales management.

EDUCATION:

University of Pittsburgh, Pittsburgh, PA

Bachelor of Arts in Economics
Expected June 2000

HONORS:

Pitt Honorary Scholar
Pennsylvania Honor Society
Freshman Economics Scholarship, 1998

ACTIVITIES:

Student Government
Freshman Advisor
Homecoming Planning Committee
Basketball Team

WORK EXPERIENCE:

Nabisco, Inc., Philadelphia, PA

Sales Intern, 1999
Assisted sales staff in research, demographics, sales forecasts, identifying new customers, and promotion.

University of Pittsburgh, Pittsburgh, PA

General Office, Registrar, 1997
Processed transcript requests. Entered registrations on the computer. Provided information to students.

SPECIAL SKILLS:

Able to translate Spanish. Experience using Microsoft Word, Excel, and Access software programs.

REFERENCES:

Available on request.

REVA POPERMAN
Snadler Hall
144 Glendon Ave.
Los Angeles, CA 90289
310/555-2384

CAREER OBJECTIVE
A position in the field of Human Resources.

EDUCATION
UCLA, Los Angeles, CA
Bachelor of Arts in Business
Expected June 2000

HONORS
Phi Beta Kappa
Dean's List four semesters
Peter J. Tolbrook Award, 1998

ACTIVITIES
President, Student Government
Freshman Advisor
Homecoming Planning Committee
Volleyball Team

WORK EXPERIENCE

NBC, Inc., Burbank, CA
Human Resources Intern, 1999

Assisted Human Resources Director in personnel acquisition and evaluation. Received and filed resumes. Administered tests to prospective employees. Set up appointments for interviews.

UCLA, Los Angeles, CA
Research/Office Assistant, 1997 - 1998

Researched and compiled materials for department professors. Arranged filing system and supervisor's library. Organized department inventory.

SPECIAL SKILLS

Fluent in Spanish. Experience using FileMaker Pro and Microsoft Word.

REFERENCES AVAILABLE ON REQUEST.

PEREGRINE C. WATERS
33301 Rondo Dr.
Tempe, AZ 77799
602/555-3920
602/555-2222

OBJECTIVE

A management position in an accounting firm.

SKILLS & ACCOMPLISHMENTS

- Handled yearly and quarterly accruals and reconciliations.
- Processed several hundred invoices per day.
- Supervised several employees.
- Oversaw up to 50 vendor adjustments and inquiries per day.
- Monitored expenses.
- Processed and routed checks.
- Audited vendor invoices for payment.
- Handled vendor inquiries and adjustments.
- Oversaw bookkeeping, check requests, and disbursements.
- Billed invoices.
- Handled accounts receivable and accounts payable.

EMPLOYMENT HISTORY

BULLOCK'S, Tempe, AZ
Accounts Payable Supervisor, 1994 - present

PETERS, INC., Sante Fe, NM
Accounts Payable Manager, 1989 - 1994

PECKER'S FOODS, INC., Sacramento, CA
Assistant Manager, Accounts Payable, 1981 - 1988

AMERICA WEST, INC., Provo, UT
Billing Coordinator, 1977 - 1981

EDUCATION

TEMPE COMMUNITY COLLEGE, Tempe, AZ
Attended night classes, 1989 - 1990
Studied accounting and advanced accounting.

HANOVER HIGH SCHOOL, Fort Dix, SC
Earned diploma, 1976
Concentration in mathematics

REFERENCES PROVIDED ON REQUEST.

LUIS CASTILLO

8155 N. Knox
Skokie, IL 60076
708/555-3168

WORK EXPERIENCE:

Gateway, Inc., Chicago, IL

Manager/Salesman, 11/98 - present
Managed own jewelry business. Sold jewelry at wholesale and retail levels. Negotiated prices with customers. Handled all finances and bookkeeping.

West Miami Jewelry, Miami, FL

Manager, 1/97 - 11/98
Managed a retail jewelry store. Oversaw all aspects of sales, purchasing, and bookkeeping. Supervised two employees.

Pelencho Travel, Chicago, IL

Travel Consultant, 4/93 - 1/97
Sold airline tickets and tour packages. Advised customers on travel plans. Handled ARC reports to airline corporations.

EDUCATION:

Interamerica Business Institute, Chicago, IL

2/99 - present
Major: Business Management

New World Institute, Chicago, IL

1992 - 1993
Certificate, Travel Consultant

Northeastern University, Chicago, IL

Attended 1991 - 1993
Area of concentration: Business Management

References available on request.

EUGENE HARRIS

2900 Greynolds St.

Deltona, FL 32725

(813) 555-2929

SKILLS & ACHIEVEMENTS:

- Developed and installed financial structure and controls of a new company, which facilitated the sale of the business at a substantial profit within six years.

- Directed the design and installation of a computerized financial reporting system for a growth company without any increase in personnel.

- Supervised the design and installation of a tied-in standard cost system that identified scrap and labor variances, thereby saving $200,000.

- Strengthened inventory controls that resulted in a $260,000 decrease in inventory and minimal inventory adjustments.

- Decreased accounting staff 20 percent by converting manual posting to computerized job-order system.

- Originated a "sound alarm" bulletin that tracked percentage-of-completion of jobs, thereby controlling costs.

- Reduced auditing fees 15 percent by initiating a procedure for preparation schedules for year-end working papers.

- Initiated and installed financial procedures for a highly profitable turnaround situation.

EMPLOYMENT HISTORY:

Finance Director 1991 - present	Amalgamated Systems Miami, FL
Controller 1986 - 1991	Charles T. Murrow, Inc. New York, NY
Controller/Treasurer 1975 - 1985	The Morris Company Detroit, MI
Controller 1968 - 1975	Adams Cable, Inc. Detroit, MI
Staff Accountant 1963 - 1968	Reva & Reva, Inc. Peoria, IL

Page 1 of 2

EDUCATION:

Baruch College of City University, Peoria, IL
B.A. in Accounting, 1962

Pace University, Detroit, MI
Computer Studies Certificate, 1985

REFERENCES:

Furnished on request.

LINDA S. WOODS
3302 Harbor Drive South
#4554
Ft. Lauderdale, FL 33020
305/555-8903
305/555-9000
swoods@ix.com

WORK EXPERIENCE

South Florida Boat Co., Miami, FL

District Sales Manager, 1994 - present
Planned successful strategies to identify and develop new accounts. Increased sales by at least 20 percent each year (45 percent in 1996). Researched and analyzed market conditions to seek out new customers. Developed weekly and monthly sales strategies. Supervised seven sales representatives.

Miami Freight, Inc., Miami, FL

Account Executive, 1992 - 1994
Handled sales accounts for southern Florida area. Expanded customer base by 25 percent during my tenure. Conducted field visits to solve customer complaints. Maintained daily contact with customers by telephone to ensure good customer/company relations. Wrote product information flyers and distributed them through a direct-mail plan.

Harrison Pandy, Inc., Denver, CO

Sales Representative, 1991 - 1992
Sold and serviced office copiers to businesses and schools in the greater Denver area. Maintained good customer relations through frequent contact. Identified potential customers for management.

EDUCATION

University of Colorado, Boulder, CO

B.A., 1991
Major: Economics
Minor: Music
G.P.A. 3.3/4.0

PROFESSIONAL MEMBERSHIPS

South Florida Sales Association, Treasurer, 1996 - 1998
Miami Chamber of Commerce, 1994 - present

REFERENCES

Available on request.

SARAH RESSENELAR
1202 W. North Ave.
Chicago, IL 60645
312/555-8908
312/555-7200

OBJECTIVE:

Retail management.

WORK EXPERIENCE:

GANDY'S SHOES, CHICAGO, IL

Assistant Manager, 1995 - present

Served as assistant manager of a quality shoe store with partial supervision of seven salespeople. Researched customers' buying habits and preferences. Handled promotion and mailings for special sales and in-store events. Helped to increase sales through personal attention to customer needs.

FLAHERTY JEWELERS, ARLINGTON HEIGHTS, IL

Salesperson, 1988 - 1995

Sold jewelry at a fine jewelry store. Greeted customers and advised them on their needs. Generated repeat business by encouraging customers to return. Entered data on computer to keep track of inventory. Handled returns and orders from distributor. Designed displays for store.

CANON CO., ATLANTA, GA

Sales Representative, 1983 - 1988

Sold and serviced office copiers to businesses and schools in the greater Atlanta area. Maintained good customer relations through frequent calls and visits. Identified potential customers.

EDUCATION:

Atlanta Community College, Atlanta, GA
Attended two years. Majored in business.

Central High School, Marietta, GA
Graduated 1982. Won math award.

REFERENCES:

Available on request.

RAMON HERVEZ

4742 N. Lawndale

Chicago, IL 60625

312/555-2574

OBJECTIVE:

Manager of Wood's Video Store.

WORK EXPERIENCE:

Wood's Video, Chicago, IL

Assistant Manager, 1995 - present
Served as assistant manager of a full-service video store with partial supervision of five salespeople. Researched customers' buying habits and preferences. Handled promotion and mailings for special sales and in-store events. Helped to increase sales through personal attention to customer needs.

Johnson Florists, Chicago, IL

Salesperson, 1988 - 1995
Sold flowers. Greeted customers and advised them on their needs. Generated repeat business by encouraging customers to return. Entered data on computer to keep track of inventory. Handled returns and orders from distributor. Designed displays for store.

Mita Co., Chicago, IL

Sales Representative, 1983 - 1988
Sold and serviced office copiers to businesses and schools in the greater Chicago area. Maintained good customer relations through frequent calls and visits. Identified potential customers.

EDUCATION:

Northeastern Illinois University, Chicago, IL

Attended two years.
Majored in business.

Central High School, Chicago, IL

Graduated 1983.
Won math award.

REFERENCES:

Available on request.

Peter Simmons

678 Park Street #546
Noblesville, IN 46060
pesimm@aol.com

OBJECTIVE:

To obtain an executive position in marketing with an emerging company that is dedicated to a long-term program.

EXPERIENCE:

5/98 - Present   DCS SOFTWARE, INC., Noblesville, IN
Senior Partner
Contingency marketing agency

- Designed marketing strategies for local and national companies
- Directly responsible for meeting payroll of 25 full-time employees
- Improved sales for one company by over 25 percent in a 12-month period
- Developed marketing programs for corporations

1/97 - 5/98   BLAUVELT ENGINEERS, New York, NY
Regional Sales Manager
Business communications systems

- Set regional sales record in six months
- Procured ten national accounts
- Exceeded company goals for the 1997 fiscal year
- Developed sales marketing program for the northwest regional area

8/93 - 1/97   EDWARDS AND KELCEY, Livingston, NJ
Marketing Director

- Implemented international marketing program
- Promoted from sales executive to marketing director
- Company's sales increased over 100 percent in a 12-month span
- Successful in developing database and reselling directly

EDUCATION:

Stevens Institute of Technology, Hoboken, NJ
Bachelor of Arts degree in Technical Marketing Design, 1993

MEGAN T. PHILLIPS

4332 S. Bridgefield Lane
San Diego, CA 92138
619/555-3472
619/555-3678

JOB OBJECTIVE:

A challenging position where I can put my knowledge and experience to work by combining high-volume selling of major accounts with an administrative ability that increases sales through the development of an effective sales force.

EMPLOYMENT HISTORY:

Tribor Industries, San Diego, CA

Regional Sales Manager, 1993 - present
Managed sales of various product lines in western markets for a leading producer of high-quality linens. Represented several corporate divisions of a company with sales in excess of $3,000,000 annually. Directed and motivated a sales team of 12 representatives in planned selling to achieve and surpass company goals.

Tribor Industries, San Diego, CA

District Manager, 1988 - 1993
Acted as sales representative for the San Diego metropolitan area. Expanded wholesale and dealer distribution by 80 percent during my tenure. Promoted to Regional Sales Manager after five years' service.

American Office Supply, Chicago, IL

Assistant to Sales Manager, 1984 - 1988
Handled internal and external sales and marketing, including samples, advertising, and pricing. Served as company sales representative and sold a range of office supplies to retail stores.

EDUCATION:

University of Michigan, Ann Arbor, MI

B.A. Business Administration, 1983
Major Field: Management

SEMINARS:

National Management Association Seminar, 1992
Purdue University Seminars, 1995, 1996

PROFESSIONAL MEMBERSHIPS:

Sales and Marketing Association of San Diego
National Association of Market Developers

REFERENCES:

Available upon request.

MARION THERESA OPPEREN
2301 E. 5th St.
Seattle, WA 99999
206/555-2900 (Day)
206/555-2810 (Evening)
cobby@freenet.com

OBJECTIVE: Personnel administration.

SKILLS & ACHIEVEMENTS

LABOR RELATIONS
- Oversaw all labor relations between the corporation and the union.
- Worked with the personnel department to plan labor policy, negotiate contracts, review hiring practices, and maintain records.
- Participated on grievance committees. Advised Vice President of Personnel on legal matters.
- Supervised a staff of ten employees.

PERSONNEL ADMINISTRATION
- Supervised a staff of eight interviewers and testers for hiring of office and warehouse personnel.
- Assisted Personnel Manager with all department operations.
- Oversaw all records for warehouse personnel.
- Developed a successful training and evaluation program for all company employees.

EMPLOYMENT HISTORY

Teledine Electronics, Inc., Seattle, WA
Industrial Relations Manager, 1993 - present

Peperillo's Pasta Co., Chicago, IL
Assistant Personnel Manager, 1988 - 1993

George Noffs Storage Co., Chicago, IL
Administrative Intern, 1987 - 1988

EDUCATION

University of Illinois, Urbana, IL
Juris Doctor, 1988
Admitted to the Illinois Bar Association, 1988

Kansas College, Wichita, KS
B.S. in Management, 1984

REFERENCES

Provided on request.

SARA STEVENS

332 E. Geobert Rd.

Terre Haute, IN 48930

317/555-3890

JOB OBJECTIVE:

Manager of a flower shop.

WORK EXPERIENCE:

TERRY'S FLOWERS, Terre Haute, IN

Assistant Sales Manager, 1997 - present
Sold flowers, waited on customers, filled phone orders, handled special orders, and designed window displays. Handled the placing of ads for a major advertising campaign. Represented store at conventions.

AVANT BOOKS, Indianapolis, IN

Retail Clerk, 1995 - 1996
Sold books to customers, filled special orders, and arranged inventory. Handled customer returns and special requests.

EDUCATION:

REVERS HIGH SCHOOL, Indianapolis, IN

Graduated June 1997

Ranked 15th in a class of 250

Worked in student bookstore for four years

REFERENCES:

Available on request.

GEORGE PASTERNECK
1119 S. Figueroa Ave.
Miami, FL 33303
305/555-6766
pasterneck@aol.com

OBJECTIVE

A management position in a large finance company.

EDUCATION

University of Miami, Miami, FL

Graduate School of Business Administration
M.B.A. expected June 2000
Concentration: Finance
Finance Club
Student Advisory Board

Boston University, Boston, MA

B.A. in Economics, 1997
Summa Cum Laude
Phi Beta Kappa
Student Government Vice President

WORK EXPERIENCE

Studebaker & Bostwick, Miami, FL

Financial Accounting Intern, 1999
Participated in standard accounting, credit approval, budgeting, and variance analysis. Handled bank balances and money management.

First Florida Bank, Ft. Lauderdale, FL

Commercial Loan Intern, 1998
Oversaw accounts in the automated teller system. Provided financial data to commercial account officers. Handled the collection of arrears.

Boston University, Boston, MA

Assistant, Accounts Payable Department, 1997 - 1998
Assisted with bookkeeping, check requests, and disbursements. Billed invoices. Tracked accounts receivable and accounts payable.

REFERENCES AVAILABLE UPON REQUEST.

REBECCA ROBINSON

1801 Kirchoff Rd.
Rolling Meadows, IL 60007
708/555-3839
rebrob@earthlink.net

JOB OBJECTIVE

Public relations director for Hot Fun Sunglasses Co.

ACCOMPLISHMENTS & ACHIEVEMENTS

- Managed a sales/marketing staff that included account managers and sales representatives.
- Represented company to clients and retailers.
- Monitored and studied the effectiveness of a national distribution network.
- Organized and planned convention displays and strategy.
- Designed and executed direct-mail campaign that identified marketplace needs and new options for products.
- Oversaw all aspects of sales/marketing budget.
- Conceived ads, posters, and point-of-purchase materials for products.
- Initiated and published a monthly newsletter that was distributed to current and potential customers.
- Handled design and programming for www.hotfunsunglasses.com website.

WORK HISTORY

Hot Fun Sunglasses Co., Schaumburg, IL

National Sales Manager, 1996 - present

Account Manager, 1994 - 1996

Assistant Account Manager, 1993 - 1994

Research Assistant, 1991 - 1993

Secretary, 1987 - 1991

EDUCATION

Indiana University, Bloomington, IN

B.A. in Economics, 1987

SEMINARS

National Marketing Association Seminars, 1994 - 1998

SPECIAL SKILLS

Computer programming experience, including HTML, database, and spreadsheet skills.

REFERENCES AVAILABLE.

REBA MALONEY
331 Maple Ave.
Seattle, WA 99449
206/555-3893 (Home)
206/555-4444 (Work)

OBJECTIVE

A management position at a dress shop.

WORK EXPERIENCE

AVON DRESS SHOP, Seattle, WA

Assistant Sales Manager, 1998 - present

Sold dresses, waited on customers, advised on style, handled special orders and mail orders, and took care of returned merchandise. Assisted in the design of window displays. Oversaw the placement of ads for a major advertising campaign. Represented store at conventions.

QUALITY BOUTIQUE, Tall Oaks, WA

Salesperson, 1996 - 1997

Sold accessories to customers, filled special orders, organized and arranged inventory. Handled customer returns and special requests. Designed window displays.

EDUCATION

TALL OAKS HIGH SCHOOL, Tall Oaks, WA

Graduated June 1997
Ranked 14th in a class of 300
Worked in student bookstore four years
Tennis team

REFERENCES

Provided on request.

JOHN JAMES HYMAN III
5555 Euclid Avenue
Ft. Lauderdale, FL 33053
305/555-8982 (Day)
305/555-6001 (Evening)

OBJECTIVE: A management position with a machine tool manufacturer where I can apply my abilities and experience in sales and marketing.

WORK EXPERIENCE:

Florida Hydraulics, Inc., Miami, FL
Assistant Sales Manager, January 1994 - present

Managed a staff of seven sales representatives. Supervised the production of a marketing newsletter that has circulation throughout the company. Cowrote the annual marketing plan. Served as a liaison between sales staff and upper management.

Peaston Machine Tools, Inc., Tampa, FL
Sales Representative, March 1991 - November 1993

Sold machine tools to business and industry. Wrote articles on sales techniques for monthly newsletter. Handled seven accounts in which sales rose 29 percent during my tenure.

EDUCATION:

B.S. in Civil Engineering
Miami University, Miami, FL, 1990

PROFESSIONAL MEMBERSHIPS:

Society of Civil Engineers, New York, NY
1992 - present

Machine Tools Sales Organization, Chicago, IL
1993 - present

SPECIAL SKILLS: Fluent in Spanish and French.

REFERENCES: Available on request.

JOE CAMPOVERDE

9000 N. Evergreen St.
Little Rock, AR 22902
501/555-3168

JOB OBJECTIVE:

A position as a travel consultant with a long-term goal of management.

WORK EXPERIENCE:

Terrace Travel, Little Rock, AR

Travel Consultant, 1996 - present
Sold airline tickets and tour packages. Advised customers on travel plans. Handled ARC reports to airline corporations.

Joe's Jewelry, Inc., Little Rock, AR

Manager/Salesman, 1994 - 1996
Managed own jewelry business. Sold jewelry at wholesale and retail levels. Negotiated prices with customers. Handled all finances and bookkeeping.

Savannah Jewelry, Savannah, GA

Manager, 1993 - 1994
Managed a retail jewelry store. Oversaw all aspects of sales, purchasing, and bookkeeping. Supervised two employees.

EDUCATION:

International Travel School, Little Rock, AR

1995 - 1996
Certificate, Travel Consultant

Savannah University, Savannah, GA

Attended 1990 - 1992
Area of concentration: business management

SPECIAL SKILLS:

Hands-on experience using System One and Sabre.

References available on request.

MICHELLE WOODS
1201 W. Porter Ave.
Oak Park, IL 60302
708/555-9000
708/555-9492

OBJECTIVE

Vice President of Operations at Osco Drug Co.

WORK EXPERIENCE

Osco Drug Co., Oak Park, IL
Manager of Operations, 1990 - present
Supervised marketing, production, distribution, and accounting. Introduced and developed a computer system to provide accurate inventory controls. Achieved efficiency savings of over $100,000 during system's first year of operation.

Osco Drug Co., Oak Park, IL
Product Manager, 1988 - 1990
Initiated several new products that resulted in high profit margins for the company. Coordinated research, production, and promotional programs. Introduced new packaging concepts.

Osco Drug Co., Oak Park, IL
Regional Sales Manager, 1986 - 1988
Supervised 34 brokers and salespeople. Increased sales 40 percent through special marketing programs. Developed better customer distribution at lower costs.

Osco Drug Co., Oak Park, IL
District Manager, 1985 - 1986
Handled sales in Chicago area. Increased profits 19 percent in my first year. Promoted to Regional Manager after one year.

Jewel Food Stores, Inc., Melrose Park, IL
Sales Representative, 1982 - 1985
Sold to wholesalers and chain stores in the Midwest. Opened many new accounts that previous sales representatives could not open.

OTHER ACHIEVEMENTS

Marketing consultant for private businesses.
Wrote a book on product efficiency.
Contributed to various trade journals.

EDUCATION

University of Michigan, Ann Arbor, MI

B.S., 1980
Major in business, minor in economics

Attended seminars at Simmons Institute, Cleveland, OH, and J. L. Kellogg School of Management, Evanston, IL

PROFESSIONAL MEMBERSHIPS

National Management Association
Lion's Club, Board of Directors
Midwest Sales Affiliates

REFERENCES

Available upon request.

JUAN C. GARCIA
2103 Afton Street
Temple Hill, Maryland 20748
Home (301) 555-2419

EDUCATION:

Columbia University, *New York, NY*
Majors: Business, Philosophy
Degree expected: Bachelor of Arts, 2000
Grade point average: 3.0
Regents Scholarship recipient
Columbia University Scholarship recipient

EXPERIENCE:

7/99 - 9/99   Graduate Business Library, Columbia University, NY
General library duties. Entered new students and books into computer system. Gave out microfiche. Reserved and distributed materials.

9/98 - 5/99   German Department, Columbia University, NY
Performed general office duties. Offered extensive information assistance by phone and in person. Collated and proofread class materials. Assisted professors in the gathering of class materials.

6/98 - 9/98   Loan Collections Department, Columbia University, NY
Initiated new filing system for the office. Checked arrears in Bursar's Office during registration period.

9/97 - 5/98   School of Continuing Education, Columbia University, NY
Involved in heavy public contact as well as general clerical duties.

SPECIAL ABILITIES:

Fluent in Spanish. Currently studying German. Can program in Virtual Basic. Excellent research skills.

REFERENCES:

Available on request.

SANDRA L. PEARSON

12 E. Tenth St.

San Francisco, CA 94890

415/555-2343

JOB OBJECTIVE

A management position in cable television advertising sales.

RELEVANT EXPERIENCE

- Sold space in television for four major clients in the automotive industry.
- Served as a liaison between clients and television and radio station salespeople.
- Researched demographic and public buying habits for clients.
- Sold space for daytime programming on local TV station.
- Advised station on content and suitability of ads.
- Served as a liaison between station and those purchasing advertising space.

EMPLOYMENT HISTORY

Medialink Advertising Agency, San Francisco, CA
Television Space Sales, September 1993 - June 2000.

KTUT Television, Portland, OR
Television Space Sales, October 1991 - August 1993.

KFTF Radio, Berkeley, CA
Staff Sales Assistant, June 1989 - June 1991.

EDUCATION

B.A. in Communications, University of California at Berkeley, 1991.

HONORS

Seeger Award, Outstanding Communications Senior, 1991

Dean's List, five semesters

Salutatorian, Overland High School, Palo Alto, CA, 1987

REFERENCES PROVIDED ON REQUEST.

THEODORE WELLINGTON
34 W. Washington Drive
New York, NY 10019
212/555-4904

JOB OBJECTIVE

A senior management position in sales and marketing.

RELEVANT ACHIEVEMENTS

- Introduced new and existing product lines through presentations to marketing directors.
- Developed new products, which resulted in increased sales.
- Increased sales from $3 million to $12 million during the past six years.
- Supervised five sales agencies throughout the United States and Canada.
- Developed fifteen new accounts.
- Researched the market to coordinate product line with current trends.
- Increased company's share of the market through improved quality products.
- Oversaw programming and development of company website.

EMPLOYMENT HISTORY

Surf City Skateboard Co., New York, NY

Vice President of Sales and Marketing, 1987 - present

Nike, Inc., San Bernardino, CA

Sales and Product Manager, 1982 - 1987

Vons Ltd., Los Angeles, CA

Sales Representative, 1977 - 1982

EDUCATION

University of Southern California, Los Angeles, CA

B.S. in Marketing, 1975

SEMINARS

Manhattan Sales & Marketing Seminar, 1995 - 1998

National Marketing Association, 1996 - 1997

Webnoize, 1999

REFERENCES

Provided on request.

LEONARD PHILLIP SCHROEDER

1550 W. Harbor Drive

Chicago, IL 60614

312/555-1434 (Day)

312/555-3333 (Night)

JOB OBJECTIVE

Marketing manager for a company that manufactures auto parts.

PROFESSIONAL EXPERIENCE

Marketing

- Researched competitive products to evaluate competitors' strengths and weaknesses.
- Planned a marketing strategy that resulted in a significant increase in accounts.
- Maintained demographic data to ascertain buyer profile.

Sales and Promotion

- Made cold calls and visits to sporting goods retailers, which resulted in increased accounts.
- Visited and serviced existing accounts to encourage continued sales.
- Advised customers on options available to meet a wide range of product needs.
- Handled dealer requests for information and sample products.

EMPLOYMENT HISTORY

Sears Automotive, Inc., Chicago, IL
Assistant Sales Manager, 1993 - present
Sales Representative, 1991 - 1993

Teychert Co., Chicago, IL
Marketing Assistant, 1990

Royal Crown Cola, Inc., Cicero, IL
Salesperson, 1988 - 1990

Baker's Square Restaurant, Lincolnwood, IL
Waiter, 1987 - 1988

EDUCATION

Southern Illinois University, Carbondale, IL

B.A. in Marketing, 1990

HONORS

Phi Beta Kappa, 1990

Dean's List, 1988 - 1990

Harrison Marketing Scholarship Recipient, 1988, 1989

President, Student Activities Board, 1990

SPECIAL SKILLS

Experience using a variety of word processing, database, and spreadsheet software. Knowledge of German and French.

REFERENCES

Provided on request.

DARREN SCHWARZWALTER
1001 Park Avenue
New York, NY 11201
212/555-1113
darrens@aol.com

JOB SOUGHT

A position in circulation management within the publishing field.

WORK EXPERIENCE

PARKER PUBLISHING CO., NEW YORK, NY

Circulation Director, 1997 - present

Developed and implemented all circulation and related programs. Devised and coordinated merchandise marketing promotions. Oversaw subscription promotion, direct response, graphics buying, fulfillment, E-commerce, budgets, agency sales, and newsstand sales.

NORTHEAST MAGAZINE, WHITE PLAINS, NY

Circulation Director, 1991 - 1997

Directed all circulation areas, direct response programs, agency sales, subscription programs, budgets, and fulfillment. Assisted in advertising and promotion.

OMNI MAGAZINE, NEW YORK, NY

Assistant Circulation Director, 1988 -1991

Assisted Circulation Director in circulation, including subscription promotion, newsstand, fulfillment, budgets, and direct-response programs.

SARRIS & SARRIS PUBLISHING, NEW YORK, NY

Assistant Operations Manager, 1984 - 1987

Assisted in magazine, book, direct-mail, and merchandise fulfillment services.

EDUCATION

Forest College, Forest Lawn, NY

B.A. in English, 1983

Forest College School of Business Administration

Forest Lawn, NY, 1984

REFERENCES PROVIDED UPON REQUEST.

GEORGE T. SNOW

87 Ichiban Ave.
Fairbanks, AK 99191
907/555-4951

JOB OBJECTIVE: Banquet Manager.

SKILLS & ACCOMPLISHMENTS:

FOOD SERVICES

- Directed all kitchen activities.
- Coordinated meal preparation for banquets.
- Planned menus in conjunction with banquet hosts.
- Interacted with caterers.
- Served as liaison to union officials.
- Oversaw parking arrangements for banquets.

MANAGEMENT

- Interviewed and trained kitchen and waitstaffs.
- Planned work schedules.
- Ordered all food and beverages.
- Maintained emergency backup staff.
- Designed and maintained budgets.

EMPLOYMENT HISTORY:

Fairbanks Feast, Fairbanks, AK
Restaurant Manager, 1991 - present
Assistant Restaurant Manager, 1988 - 1991

James Restaurant, Morrison Hotel, Provo, UT
Assistant Director, 1985 - 1987
Waiter, 1983 - 1985

EDUCATION:

Provo Junior College, Provo, UT
A.S. in Food Service, 1981

References furnished upon request.

PAMELA SUE HUSPERS
pshuspers@broadnet.com

Permanent Address: Temporary Address:
24 South East Hollow Road   150 Fort Washington Ave.
Berlin, NY 10951   New York, NY 10032
(518) 555-6057   (212) 738-2498

OBJECTIVE:
A management trainee position in the telecommunications industry.

EDUCATION:
Bachelor of Science, Communications

New York University, New York, NY

Date of Graduation, May 1999

Communications G.P.A. 3.45

Academic G.P.A. 3.07

PROFESSIONAL EXPERIENCE:
V.I.T.A. (Volunteer Income Tax Assistance), Spring 1999
Provided income tax assistance to lower-income and elderly taxpayers who were unable to prepare returns or pay for professional assistance.

Tutor, self-employed, September 1997 - present
Helped students to better understand the basic concepts and ideas of mathematics.

Randy's Seafood, New York, NY
Cook, Summer 1997

Prepared and cooked assorted seafood dishes. Accounted for deliveries and receiving.

Jones Construction, Brooklyn, NY
General Laborer and Driver, Summer 1995 - 1996

Operated heavy machinery and handled other responsibilities including delivering materials to and from various job sites.

ACTIVITIES AND HONORS:
Beta Alpha Psi (Communications Honor Society), 1999

Dean's List, Fall 1997 & Spring 1999

A.I.S.E.C. - Association for International Business

Racquetball and tennis teams

REFERENCES:
Available upon request.

DANIEL KEYS

548 W. Hollywood Way
Burbank, CA 91505
818/555-9090

PROFESSIONAL OBJECTIVE:

An upper-level management position in the record industry where I can employ my sales, marketing, and promotion experience.

PROFESSIONAL BACKGROUND:

Warner Bros. Records, Burbank, CA
Director of Marketing/Jazz Department, 1997 - present
Developed and implemented strategic marketing plans for new releases and catalog. Produced reissue packages and samplers, both retail and promotional. Created ad copy. Interfaced with creative services, national/local print & radio, and Internet sites. Oversaw all aspects of sales. Coordinated promotional activities and chart reports.

Immortal Records, Los Angeles, CA
National Sales Manager, 1993 - 1997
West Coast Sales Manager, 1989 - 1993
Increased sales profile, specifically West Coast retailers, one-stops, and racks. Promoted to National Sales Manager where I established sales and promotion programs for the company. Coordinated radio/chart reports.

Specialty Records, Scranton, PA
Sales Representative, 1988
Handled sales, merchandising, and account servicing for LPs and cassettes. Called on major chains and small independent retailers. Promoted new releases and maintained account inventory.

Tower Records, Los Angeles, CA
Manager, 1986 - 1987
Handled sales, merchandising, customer service, product selection and ordering, personnel management, and supervision for a full-line retail outlet.

MCA Records Distribution, Universal City, CA
Sales Representative, 1982 - 1986
Promoted and sold MCA products to Los Angeles and surrounding counties. Designed in-store and window displays. Coordinated media advertising support programs.

EDUCATION:

Berkeley University, Berkeley, CA
B.A., Liberal Arts, 1980

References provided on request.

KRISTINE HINCH

5222 38th St.
Washington, DC 20013
202/555-2003

OBJECTIVE: Personnel Management.

WORK EXPERIENCE:

Avery Publishing Company, San Francisco, CA

Payroll Specialist, 1992 - present
Determine job grading system. Evaluate jobs. Maintain employee budget. Conduct performance appraisals. Decide wage increases and adjustments. Set salary ranges. Write job descriptions. Coordinate compensation surveys. Gather data on vacations, sick time, and leaves of absence.

EDUCATION:

University of California at Santa Barbara

Bachelor's Degree in Economics, 1991

Personnel Management Institute

Harrison University, Seattle, WA
Summer 1997

HONORS:

UCSB Economics Scholarship, 1988 - 1989

Elected Student Government Treasurer, 1990

Gamma Kappa Phi Honorary Society, 1990 - 1991

REFERENCES:

Available upon request.

JOHANNA FARAC

152 S. Fedner Drive
Omaha, NE 73802
402/555-9000 (Day)
402/555-6712 (Evening)

JOB OBJECTIVE

A position as a management trainee with a major bookstore retail chain
selling to all trade areas.

WORK EXPERIENCE

Crown Books, Inc., Omaha, NE

Assistant Sales Manager, 1997 - present

Sold books, waited on customers, filled mail orders, handled special
orders, and took care of returned merchandise. Contributed to window
displays. Handled the placing of ads for a major advertising campaign.
Represented store at conventions.

Fern Books, Fernwood, NE

Salesperson, 1995 - 1996

Sold books to customers, filled special orders, organized and arranged
inventory. Handled customer complaints and special requests.

EDUCATION

Omaha High School, Omaha, NE

Graduated June 1997

Ranked 12th in a class of 320

Worked in student bookstore four years

REFERENCES

Provided on request.

YOLANDA RICHARDS

6600 Manhattan Ave.
Brooklyn, NY 10090
718/555-9656
yolanda@focuslens.com

JOB OBJECTIVE:

Vice President of Focus Lens, Inc.

PROFESSIONAL EXPERIENCE:

Focus Lens, Inc., New York, NY
Regional Manager, 1992 - present

Sold custom-designed point-of-purchase elements and product displays. Researched target areas and developed new account leads. Placed advertising in national publications and on websites. Made sales presentations to potential customers. Participated in lens industry trade shows.

Redheart Lawn Co., Forest Lawn, NY
District Sales Manager, 1989 - 1991

Planned successful sales strategies to identify and develop new accounts. Supervised seven sales representatives. Increased sales by at least 20 percent in each of my four years. Researched and analyzed market conditions to seek out new customers. Wrote monthly sales reports.

Ace Office Supply Co., Brooklyn, NY
Account Executive, 1986 - 1989

Managed accounts in the New York metropolitan area. Expanded customer base 30 percent in four years. Maintained daily contact with customers by telephone to ensure good customer/company relations. Wrote product information flyers and distributed them through a direct-mail program.

EDUCATION:

Northwestern University, Evanston, IL
M.B.A. with honors, 1985

Drake University, Des Moines, IA
B.A. in Accounting, 1982

PROFESSIONAL MEMBERSHIPS:

Brooklyn Sales Association, 1991 - present
New York Merchants Group, 1989 - present

REFERENCES:

Available upon request.

CAROLYN JAMESON
6900 Market St. #455
San Francisco, CA 91009
415/555-2990
415/555-3939

EMPLOYMENT OBJECTIVE:

A management position in an American/Continental restaurant in the greater San Francisco area.

EMPLOYMENT HISTORY:

Le Boufant, San Francisco, CA
Assistant Manager, 1994 - present

Assist in supervision of general food service in a 65-table restaurant. Oversee breakfast and luncheon kitchen and dining staffs. Develop menus in conjunction with the chef. Handle bookkeeping.

Hilton Hotel, Oakland, CA
Assistant Banquet Manager, 1991 - 1994

Organized and planned banquets and private parties for various business meetings, community events, wedding receptions, and other personal events. Chose meals, music, and decorations along with hosts.

Smiley's Bar & Grill, San Francisco, CA
Waitress, 1989 - 1991

EDUCATION:

American Restaurant Institute, Los Angeles, CA
Certificate in Restaurant Management, 1993

Santa Monica Junior College, Santa Monica, CA
Associate Degree in Food Services, 1988

PROFESSIONAL MEMBERSHIPS:

Bay Area Restaurant Association, 1994 - present

Neighborhood Development Council, 1996 - 1998

REFERENCES: AVAILABLE UPON REQUEST.

CARLOS ENRIQUE PENA
14 E. Bryn Mawr Ave.
Chicago, IL 60645
312/555-3849

PROFESSIONAL EXPERIENCE:

Florsheim Shoe Co., Chicago, IL
Sales Manager, 1993 - present
Sold custom-designed point-of-purchase elements and product displays. Researched target areas and developed new account leads. Placed advertising in national publications. Customized sales presentations to the specific interests of potential customers. Participated in industry trade shows and hosted trade events.

Quest Fixtures, Inc., St. Louis, MO
Regional Sales Manager, 1989 - 1993
Implemented successful sales strategies to identify and develop new accounts. Supervised seven sales representatives. Increased sales by at least 20 percent in each of my four years. Researched and analyzed market conditions to identify and recruit new customers. Created and analyzed monthly sales reports.

Carolina Freight, Raleigh, NC
Account Executive, 1986 - 1989
Effectively managed accounts in the greater Raleigh area. Expanded customer base 30 percent in four years. Maintained daily contact with customers by telephone to ensure good customer/company relations. Wrote product information flyers and distributed them to a targeted audience through a direct-mail program.

EDUCATION:

Boston University, Boston, MA
M.B.A. with honors, 1985

Western University, Phoenix, AZ
B.A. in Accounting, 1982

PROFESSIONAL MEMBERSHIPS:

Midwest Sales Association, 1994 - present
Midwest Merchants Group, 1989 - present

REFERENCES: Available upon request.

GERALD ROBERT SCAMPI

4890 W. 57th St.
New York, NY 10019
212/555-3678
scampi@atlanticrecords.com

JOB OBJECTIVE

Vice President of Promotion for a communications company.

PROFESSIONAL EXPERIENCE

1992 - present ATLANTIC RECORDS, New York, NY
Promotion Manager. Developed and executed all marketing strategy for record promotion in New York, New Jersey, and Massachusetts. Interfaced with sales department and retail stores to ensure adequate product placement. Attended various company-sponsored sales, marketing, and management seminars.

1982 - 1991 IRS RECORDS, Studio City, CA
Promotion Manager. Planned all marketing strategy for record promotions in the southeast United States. Worked closely with sales and touring bands to ensure product visibility in the marketplace.

1980 - 1982 WLS RADIO, Chicago, IL
Morning DJ. Played CHR music. Made TV appearances and public events appearances for the station. Organized and staffed station's news department. Promoted to Music Director after one year.

1975 - 1980 WGLT RADIO, Atlanta, GA
Served as Program Director, Music Director, and News Director during my tenure.

EDUCATION

COLUMBIA COLLEGE, Chicago, IL
Attended 1974 - 1975
Studied audio engineering.

REFERENCES AVAILABLE ON REQUEST.

WILLIAM ROBERT GARRETT

5050 W. Palatine Road
Palatine, IL 60067
708/555-3789 (Home)
708/555-1000 (Work)
bill.microtech@att.net

JOB OBJECTIVE

A management-level position in computer sales where I can use my sales and technical experience in the computer industry.

RELEVANT EXPERIENCE

Sales

- Handled sales accounts for northwest suburban Chicago area.
- Expanded customer base by 25 percent during my tenure.
- Conducted field visits to solve customers' problems.
- Maintained daily contact with customers to ensure good customer/company relations.
- Wrote product information flyers and sales manual.
- Contributed content to company website.

Technical

- Installed and maintained operating system.
- Defined and oversaw network lists and tables.
- Coordinated problem solving with phone companies.
- Performance-tuned subsystems and networks.
- Planned and installed new hardware and programming techniques.

Systems Analysis

- Documented procedures for mechanization of payroll department.
- Created standards and procedures for main accounting system.
- Developed test procedures for reverification of new application.
- Developed distribution lists, user IDs, and standards for electronic mail system.

EMPLOYMENT HISTORY

MICROTECH COMPUTERS, Northbrook, IL
Account Executive, 1987 - present

APPLE COMPUTERS, Berkeley, CA
Technical Support Specialist, 1980 - 1987

DATALOG, INC., St. Louis, MO
Systems Analyst, 1969 - 1979

EDUCATION

UNIVERSITY OF CHICAGO, Chicago, IL

M.S. in Mathematics, 1967
Honors graduate

NORTHWESTERN UNIVERSITY, Evanston, IL

B.S. in Communications, 1964

PROFESSIONAL AFFILIATIONS

Computer Sales Association
Illinois Business Chapter
Citizens for a Cleaner Environment

SEMINARS

Microtech Sales Seminars
Apple Technical Workshops

REFERENCES AVAILABLE ON REQUEST.

CHRISTOPHER BERNARD SMALLS

600 W. Porter St. #5
Las Vegas, NV 89890
514/555-3893

OBJECTIVE
A position as a management trainee in a manufacturing company.

EDUCATION
University of Nevada, Las Vegas, NV
Bachelor of Science in Business
Expected June 2000

HONORS
Dean's List four semesters

Dornburn Scholarship

UNLV Undergraduate Business Award

ACTIVITIES
President, Kappa Beta Fraternity

New Student Week Committee

Homecoming Planning Committee

Captain, Tennis Team

WORK EXPERIENCE
Porter Rand & Associates, Seattle, WA
Sales Intern, 2000

Assisted sales staff in the areas of research, demographics, sales forecasts, identifying new customers, and promotion.

University of Nevada, Las Vegas, NV
Research/Office Assistant, 1998 - 1999

Researched and compiled materials for department professors. Arranged filing system and supervisor's library. Organized department inventory.

SPECIAL SKILLS
Experience using Microsoft Office 2000 software programs.

REFERENCES AVAILABLE.

GEORGIA SADEN

453 Franklin Ave.
San Diego, CA 94890
619/555-3489

OBJECTIVE

A management position in marketing where I can use my promotion and public relations experience.

WORK EXPERIENCE

JUST PASTA INC., San Diego, CA
Marketing Director, 1994 - present

Developed a successful marketing campaign for a restaurant chain. Initiated and maintained a positive working relationship with radio and print media. Implemented marketing strategies to increase sales at less profitable outlets. Designed a training program for store managers and staff.

GREAT IDEAS CARPET CLEANING CO., Dallas, TX
Marketing Representative, 1990 - 1994

Demonstrated carpet cleaners in specialty and department stores. Reported customer reactions to manufacturers. Designed flyers and advertising to promote products. Made frequent calls to retail outlets.

REBO CHIPS, INC., Chicago, IL
Assistant to Sales Manager, 1985 - 1990

Handled both internal and external areas of sales and marketing, including samples, advertising, and pricing. Served as company sales representative and sold potato chips to retail outlets.

EDUCATION

UNIVERSITY OF ILLINOIS AT CHICAGO, Chicago, IL
B.A. Marketing, 1984

SEMINARS

San Diego State Marketing Workshop, 1996, 1997
Sales and Marketing Association Seminars, 1992

REFERENCES AVAILABLE ON REQUEST.

JEFFREY CROSS

4901 Main St. #242

Evanston, IL 60202

847-555-6362

JOB OBJECTIVE

Seeking a position as manager of a housewares department of a major department store where I can use my talents as a manager and a salesperson.

ACHIEVEMENTS

Promoted from customer service representative to salesperson to assistant manager in housewares at Marshall Field's. Managed a staff of five, including hiring, job training, and supervision. Helped to reorganize inventory control methods. Assisted customers in choosing housewares and in interior design matters. Combined managerial and sales talents to increase department sales figures.

WORK EXPERIENCE

Marshall Field's, Skokie, IL

Assistant Manager, 1998 - present
Salesperson, 1996 - 1998
Customer Service Representative, 1995 - 1996

Peters Hardware, Evanston, IL

Stock Clerk, Summers 1993 - 1995

EDUCATION

Evanston High School, Evanston, IL

Graduated June 1995
Top 25 percent of class
Student Council Representative
Animal Rights Committee

Oakton Community College, Des Plaines, IL

Various night courses, including "Sales Techniques" and "Retail Management"
AHA Seminar, "Selling Housewares," 1998

REFERENCES

Provided upon request.

JANIS DARIEN

345 W. 3rd St. #42
Boston, MA 02210
Telephone: 617/555-3291
E-mail: janis@bostonu.com
Website: www.janisdarien.com

JOB OBJECTIVE: To obtain a position as a Marketing Management Trainee.

EDUCATION:

Boston University, Boston, MA
    B.A. degree in Economics, 1999
    Dean's List four quarters
    3.45 GPA in major field
    3.21 GPA overall
    Homecoming Planning Committee
Pursuing graduate studies toward a Master's degree in Marketing at Boston University, Evening Division.

Central High School, Evansville, IN
    Graduated 1995
    Top 10 percent of class
    Business manager and coordinator of student newspaper
    Vice President of senior class
    Student Council
    Pep Club

WORK EXPERIENCE:

Lewis Advertising Agency, Boston, MA
Marketing Assistant, Summer 1998

    Assisted Marketing Manager in promotion, product development, and demographic analysis.

Paterno Marketing, Boston, MA
Telephone Interviewer, Summer 1996 - 1997

White Hen Pantry, Evansville, IN
Cashier, Summer 1995

SPECIAL SKILLS: Fluent in French. Familiar with PC hardware and software.

REFERENCES: Available on request.

LYDIA REGAN BOMSON

8000 East Fifth Avenue
Silver Springs, MD 04890
202/555-8398

OBJECTIVE:

A management position in the textile manufacturing industry.

EMPLOYMENT HISTORY:

Interco., Washington, DC

Regional Sales Manager, 1991 - present
Managed sales of all product lines in eastern markets for a leading manufacturer of cotton products. Represented five corporate divisions of the company with sales in excess of $2 million annually. Directed and motivated a sales force of 12 in planned selling to achieve company goals.

Robertson Co., Miami, FL

District Manager, 1986 - 1991
Acted as sales representative for the Miami metropolitan area. Built both wholesale and dealer distribution substantially during my tenure. Developed monthly sales plans that identified necessary account maintenance and specific problems that required attention.

Western Office Products, Inc., Sarasota, FL

Assistant Sales Manager, 1977 - 1986
Handled both internal and external areas of sales and marketing, including samples, advertising, and pricing. Served as company sales representative and sold a variety of office supplies to retail stores.

EDUCATION:

Miami University, Miami, FL
B.A. in English, 1975

SEMINARS:

American Business Association Seminars, 1993 - 1998

REFERENCES:

Available on request.

MARION ZARET

3333 W. 57th St.
Apartment 12E
Brooklyn, NY 12909
718/555-2323
718/555-4999
mzaret@coke.com

OBJECTIVE:

Public relations director for soft drink company.

WORK EXPERIENCE:

Coca-Cola, Inc., New York, NY
National Sales Manager, 1995 - present
Account Manager, 1993 - 1995
Assistant Account Manager, 1992 - 1993
Personnel Assistant, 1990 - 1992
Receptionist, 1988 - 1990

Managed a sales/marketing staff that included account managers and sales representatives. Monitored and studied the effectiveness of a national distribution network. Represented company to clients and retailers in order to present new products. Organized and planned convention displays and strategy. Oversaw all aspects of sales/marketing budget. Designed and executed direct-mail program that identified marketplace needs and new options for products. Conceived ads, posters, and point-of-purchase materials for products. Initiated and published a monthly newsletter that was distributed to current and potential customers.

EDUCATION:

American University, White Plains, NY
B.A. in English, 1987

SEMINARS:

American Marketing Association Seminars, 1993 - 1998
Coca-Cola Internal Sales Workshops, 1994 - 1998
Soft Drink Industry Conventions

SPECIAL SKILLS:

Computer literate in Virtual Basic. Experience using WordPerfect and Lotus software.

REFERENCES AVAILABLE ON REQUEST.

YOSHEMA MUNO
7640 N. Redden Road
Skokie, IL 60076
708/555-3908
708/555-2300

JOB OBJECTIVE

A position as manager of a store that sells quality shoes and accessories.

WORK EXPERIENCE

Florsheim Shoes, Skokie, IL
Assistant Manager, 1995 - 1999

> Served as assistant manager of a quality shoe store with partial supervision of eight salespeople. Researched customers' buying habits and preferences. Handled promotion and mailings for special sales and in-store events. Helped to increase sales through personal attention to customer needs.

Handleman Shoe Store, Lincolnwood, IL
Salesperson, 1991 - 1995

> Sold high-quality women's shoes at an exclusive store. Named top salesperson of 1994 and 1995. Maintained a clean, attractive store area and organized inventory.

Florsheim Shoes, Chicago, IL
Salesperson, 1988 - 1991

> Sold shoes. Assisted customers in making purchase decisions. Organized and maintained stock and inventory. Helped with window displays.

EDUCATION

Stevenson Community College, Chicago, IL
> Attended two years. Majored in political science.

Calumet High School, Calumet, IL
> Graduated 1988. Won science award.

REFERENCES

Available on request.

DONALD R. CRUMP
5001 Providence St.
Washington, DC 02930
201/555-8000
201/555-3894

OBJECTIVE:

A position as marketing manager for Graphics, Inc.

PROFESSIONAL EXPERIENCE:

Burger World, Inc., Washington, DC

Marketing Director, 1992 - 1999
Developed a successful marketing campaign for a fast-food chain. Initiated and maintained a positive working relationship with radio, TV, and print media. Implemented marketing strategies to increase sales at less profitable outlets. Designed a training program for store managers and staff.

Hi Fidelity Stereo Co., Newark, NJ

Marketing Representative, 1987 - 1992
Demonstrated electronic equipment in stereo and department stores. Reported customer reactions to manufacturers. Designed flyers and advertising to promote products. Made frequent calls to retail outlets.

Interco, New York, NY

Sales Representative, 1980 - 1987
Identified clients' needs and problems and assured them of personal attention. Resolved service and billing problems. Delivered sales presentations to groups and individuals. Identified potential customers and established new accounts.

EDUCATION:

Georgetown University, Washington, DC
B.S. Evening Division, 1986
Major: Marketing
Minor: English

SEMINARS:

Washington Sales and Marketing Convention, 1997, 1998
National Marketing Association Seminar, 1989 - 1994

SPECIAL SKILLS:

Fluent in Spanish. Able to program in Virtual Basic.

REFERENCES:

Available on request.

HENRY JAZZINSKI
3000 Big Mile Road
Dallas, TX 84038
214/555-8888 (Daytime)
214/555-3839 (Evening)

OBJECTIVE

A management position in the sales and marketing field.

ACHIEVEMENTS

Sales

Increased watch sales from $3 million to $12 million during the past six years. Introduced new and existing product lines through presentations to marketing directors of major manufacturers. Developed 15 new accounts. Supervised five sales agencies throughout the United States and Canada.

Marketing

Developed new products expanding from watches to other accessories, which resulted in increased sales. Researched the watch market to coordinate product line with current fashion trends. Increased company's share of the market through improved quality products.

WORK HISTORY

Culture Shock Watch Co., Dallas, TX
Vice President of Sales and Marketing, 1988 - present

Nabisco Food Co., San Francisco, CA
Sales and Product Manager, 1983 - 1988

Avis, Inc., Los Angeles, CA
Sales Representative, 1978 - 1983

EDUCATION

University of Southern California, Los Angeles, CA
B.S. in Business Administration, 1977

SEMINARS

Dallas Sales and Marketing Seminar, 1996 - 1999
National Marketing Association, 1991 - 1993

References available on request.

RUTH M. DAVID

572 FIRST STREET
BROOKLYN, NY 11215
(212) 555-6328
ruthie@princeton.edu

Education

Princeton University, Princeton, NJ

Degree expected: M.B.A., June 2000
Class Rank: Top 25 Percent
Honors: Associate Editor, Business Journal

University of Wisconsin, Madison, WI

B.A. in Political Science, May 1998
Honors: Dean's List
Marching Band Drill Instructor, Section Leader
Residence Hall Council President

Business Experience

International Business Machines, White Plains, NY

Intern/Sales, 6/99 - 9/99
Assisted in PC Sales Division. Worked to promote distribution to retail outlets. Helped to coordinate product demonstration program used throughout the country.

Other Experience

Citizen Action Group, New York, NY

Field Manager, 6/98 - 9/98
Promoted citizen awareness of state legislative process and issues of toxic waste, utility control, and consumer legislation. Demonstrated effective fund-raising and communication methods to the canvas employees. Developed and sustained employee motivation and productivity.

University of Wisconsin, Madison, WI

Resident Assistant, Office of Residential Life, 8/96 - 5/98
Administered all aspects of student affairs in university residence halls, including program planning, discipline, and individual group counseling. Directed achievement of student goals through guidance of the residence hall council. Developed and implemented university policies.

University of Wisconsin, Madison, WI

Staff Training Lecturer, 8/97 - 11/98
Conducted workshops for residence hall staff on counseling and effective communication.

References available on request.

MATTHEW R. CLARKSON

1251 S. Maple Ave.

Des Moines, IA 52909

515/555-4999 (Day)

515/555-3429 (Evening)

OBJECTIVE:

Manager of the hardware department of a major department store.

RELEVANT ACHIEVEMENTS:

- *Promoted from customer service representative to salesperson and then to assistant manager in hardware at Sears in Des Moines.*
- *Managed a staff of six, including hiring, job training, and supervision.*
- *Helped to reorganize inventory control methods.*
- *Assisted customers in choosing and using hardware products.*
- *Combined managerial and sales talents to increase department sales.*

EMPLOYMENT HISTORY:

Sears, Des Moines, IA
> Assistant Manager, 1997 - present
> Salesperson, 1995 - 1997
> Customer Service Representative, 1994 - 1995

Sam's Hardware, West Petersville, IA
> Stock Clerk, Summers 1992 - 1994

EDUCATION:

Des Moines Township High School, Des Moines, IA
> Graduated June 1994
> Top 25 percent of class
> Student Council Secretary
> Homecoming Committee

Redbrook College, Des Moines, IA
> Various night courses, including "Retail Sales Management"
> and "Supervisory Techniques."

REFERENCES:

> Available on request.

QUENTIN PORLEAN

12½ Derbyshire Dr.
East St. Louis, IL 60989
314/555-8932

JOB SOUGHT

A position as manager of an electronics department of a major department store.

WORK EXPERIENCE

Bergstrom's, St. Louis, MO

Assistant Manager, 1998 - present
Salesperson, 1996 - 1998
Customer Service Representative, 1995 - 1996

Promoted from customer service representative to salesperson and then to assistant manager of electronics at Bergstrom's. Managed a staff of four, including hiring, job training, and supervision. Helped to reorganize inventory control methods. Assisted customers in choosing electronic products and designing entertainment centers. Combined managerial and sales talents that increased sales.

Radio Shack, East St. Louis, IL

Salesperson, Summers 1993 - 1995

Sold electronic products and equipment. Handled inventory and product orders. Assisted customers with technical questions.

EDUCATION

East St. Louis High School, East St. Louis, IL

Graduated June 1995
Top 15 percent of class
Student Council President
Black Students Alliance

Barton Community College, St. Louis, MO

Attended 1998
Courses included "Sales Techniques" and "Retail Management"
St. Louis Chamber of Commerce Retail Convention, 1998

REFERENCES

Provided on request.

DARREN TREVOL
43433 N. Melrose Ave.
Elmhurst, IL 60189
708/555-4328
708/555-1010
trevol2000@earthlink.net

OBJECTIVE:

Senior vice president of sales and marketing for Vincent Electronics, Inc.

PROFESSIONAL ACHIEVEMENTS:

Marketing

- Researched computer market to coordinate product line with current public tastes and buying trends.
- Developed new approaches to marketing software products, including in-store displays and Internet advertising.
- Organized and planned convention displays and strategies.

Sales

- Introduced new and existing product lines through presentations to major clients.
- Increased sales from $27 million to $50 million in five years.
- Initiated and developed nine new accounts.
- Supervised five sales agencies throughout the United States.

EMPLOYMENT HISTORY:

Vincent Electronics Inc., Elmhurst, IL
Sales and Marketing Manager, 1994 - present

Porcelana Inc., Melrose Park, IL
Product Coordinator, 1989 - 1994

Radio Shack, Inc., New York, NY
Sales Representative, 1984 - 1989

EDUCATION:

New York University, New York, NY
B.S. 1984
Major: Business Administration
Minor: Computer Science

REFERENCES:

Available upon request.

Sample Cover Letters

GINA STEVENSON
433 Maple Drive
Hoffman Estates, IL 60035
708/555-2341

May 23, 2001

Lisa Rice
Vice President of Personnel
Laura Ashley, Inc.
111 Commonwealth Avenue
Boston, MA 02215

Dear Ms. Rice:

I am interested in applying for the position of manager of one of your Chicago area retail stores. Enclosed are my resume and letters of recommendation.

I have been involved in retail sales for over 20 years and have gained valuable insight and experience during this time. For the past 10 years, I have been assistant sales manager at Talbot's in the Woodfield mall and also the owner and designer of my own original clothing line, "Gina Designs." My experience in women's fashion at the retail level well qualifies me for a management-level position.

The reason I am seeking employment with Laura Ashley is that I have admired and loved Laura Ashley products for many years. I feel that your stores offer the best in quality and unique women's clothing. This is why I want to be a part of your organization.

Thank you for taking the time to consider me. I look forward to hearing from you soon.

Sincerely,

Gina Stevenson

January 28, 2000

Helena Borgess
Director of Human Resources
Warner Bros., Inc.
4000 Olive Ave.
Burbank, CA 91505

Dear Ms. Borgess:

This is a letter of inquiry. I would like to know if there are any openings in your company in the Human Resources department. My area of interest is the entertainment industry and that is why I am writing to you.

I will be graduating from UCLA with a degree in Business in June of this year. Human Resources has been an area of focus in my studies, as I hope to have a career in this field. Last summer, I served as an intern in the Human Resources department at NBC, Inc., in Burbank where I assisted with personnel acquisition and evaluation, administering tests to prospective employees, and setting up appointments for interviews.

I feel that this internship helped to prepare me for a career in Human Resources within the entertainment industry.

Along with my business education and my experience in Human Resources, I also speak fluent Spanish, which I feel is a definite advantage in today's business world.

Please find my resume enclosed. You may consider me for any openings you might have. I would be happy to interview with you at your convenience.

Sincerely,

Reva Poperman
UCLA
Snadler Hall
144 Glendon Ave.
Los Angeles, CA 90289
310/555-2384

DAVID P. JENKINS
3663 N. Coldwater Canyon
North Hollywood, CA 90390
818/555-3472
818/555-3678

July 29, 2000

Mr. Jeremy Hitleman
Vice President of Sales and Marketing
Sandoval Industries
500 University Drive
Santa Barbara, CA 97809

Dear Mr. Hitleman:

I am writing to you to inquire about the possibility of obtaining a position with Sandoval
Industries as a sales/marketing manager.

My special interest in working for your company stems from a desire to expand my
experience into the area of hardware sales. Your company's recent addition of a hardware
division brought Sandoval to my attention.

Currently, I serve as regional sales manager for Tribor Industries where I represent five
corporate divisions with sales in excess of $3,000,000 annually. Previous to this position, I
served as district manager for Tribor.

I believe that my sales experience well qualifies me for a position at Sandoval Industries.
Please call me for an interview if you feel the same. Enclosed is my resume.

Sincerely,

David P. Jenkins

July 11, 2000

Scour.net
345 Maple Drive
Suite 285
Beverly Hills, CA 90210
Attn: James Soner

Dear Mr. Soner:

While visiting your website, I noticed that you are seeking a Director of Business Development for Scour.net, and I would like to have the opportunity to meet with you to discuss my interest and qualifications for this position.

For the past three years, I have managed my own Internet business, eLand, handling website development, hosting, digital imaging, and sales. Prior to that, I served as an independent Internet business consultant for a variety of companies. My resume is enclosed.

I believe I am capable of managing major activities and projects related to the pursuit of new business opportunities for Scour.net and analyzing company strategy and developing recommendations for new initiatives, alliances, and partnerships.

Please contact me at your earliest convenience so that I can meet you for an interview. I look forward to hearing from you soon.

Sincerely,

Patrick T. Koran
39392 Broad Street
Meridian, MS 39301
601-555-2929
ptk@netflash.com
www.patkoran.com

4/23/01

Harvard Peter Fendi
President
American Finance Co.
4444 E. River Drive
Detroit, MI 33393

Dear Mr. Fendi:

As a recent graduate of The Kellogg School of Business Management at Northwestern University, I am seeking a position in financial management. I met a representative of your company, Jonathon Siveva, at a recruiting seminar at Northwestern a few months ago, and he alerted me to the fact that your company would be hiring M.B.A.s this summer. Hence, this letter.

At Kellogg, my concentration was in finance. I participated in the Finance Club and served as a member of the Student Advisory Board. My practical experience includes a financial accounting internship at Thomas & Thomas, an internship in the commercial loan department at LaSalle National Bank, and a position in the accounts payable department at Northwestern.

I am enclosing my resume for a more comprehensive picture of my accomplishments and qualifications. I will contact you in the next 10 days to inquire about setting up an interview. Please feel free to contact me at the number listed below.

Sincerely,

Antonio Cruz
8925 Lake Shore Drive #442
Chicago, IL 60614
312/555-2939
antonio@nu.edu

March 23, 2001

Giuseppe Spina
Owner & General Manager
Pallermo's Restaurant
238 Market St.
San Francisco, CA 92299

Dear Mr. Spina:

I am responding to your ad in the *San Francisco Examiner* for a manager for your restaurant. Enclosed is my resume.

Since 1994, I have been the Assistant Manager at Le Boufant in San Francisco. I assist in the supervision of food service in a 65-table restaurant. I also oversee breakfast and luncheon kitchen and dining staffs. Previous to this position, I served as Assistant Banquet Manager for the Hilton Hotel in Oakland.

I have a Certificate in Restaurant Management from the American Restaurant Institute and an Associate Degree in Food Services from Santa Monica Junior College.

I am available for an interview at your convenience. I look forward to speaking with you soon.

Sincerely,

Carolyn Jameson
6900 Market St. #455
San Francisco, CA 91009
415/555-2990
415/555-3939

August 23, 2000

Steven R. Stevens
Red Man Furnace Co.
7892 Collins Ave.
Miami, FL 33102

Dear Mr. Stevens:

I am responding to your advertisement for a Sales Manager in the *Miami Herald* of August 18, 2000. I am interested in such a position, and I am forwarding my resume to you.

My sales experience is extensive and goes back ten years. As an account executive for Newmark Furnace Co., I have handled sales accounts in the south Florida area and expanded my customer base by 28 percent in the last three years. Previous to that, I worked as a sales representative for Potisco in Terre Haute, Indiana, and Honoco in Chicago, Illinois.

I feel I am qualified for the position you are currently interviewing for. If, after reviewing my resume, you feel the same, please contact me for an interview. Thank you.

Sincerely,

Patrick H. McCoy
1701 N. Hampshire Pl.
Miami, FL 33126
305/555-3909
305/555-9099

February 18, 2001

Richard Marx
Manager
Westin Hotel
1131 6th St.
Seattle, WA 98802

Dear Mr. Marx:

I am looking to break into the hotel business with a long-term goal of management. I am forwarding my resume to you with the hope that you may have an opening on your staff.

I will graduate in June of 2001 from the International School of Business in San Francisco, California, with a Certificate in Hotel Management. My previous work experience includes management of my own cookware business and management of a retail jewelry store. This work coupled with my education has prepared me for a career in hotel management.

You will find that I am reliable, hardworking, and competent. Feel free to contact me regarding an interview. Thank you for your time and consideration.

Sincerely,

Tyrell Stevenson
602 S. Texas Ave.
Oakland, CA 94611
415/555-3168
tyrell22@hotmail.com

DONALD E. THOMPSON
1314 W. Dundee Road
Buffalo Grove, IL 60006
det@microtech.com

March 30, 2000

Mr. Henry Corleone
Branch Manager Sales
Datatech Computer Co.
4444 E. Monroe
Chicago, IL 60606

Dear Mr. Corleone:

Please consider me for the position of Assistant Branch Manager of Sales at Datatech. I am enclosing my resume. I learned of this opening through *Computer Weekly* and through a colleague of mine at Microtech.

My experience in the computer industry dates back 30 years and encompasses several different areas. Most recently, I have served as Account Executive for Microtech where I handle sales accounts for the northwest suburban area. Before that, I worked for IBM in the capacity of Technical Support Specialist and Systems Analyst. I also contribute content to the Microtech website.

I believe that I could bring my expertise in these diverse areas to Datatech and thus enhance your talented sales division.

I will be calling next week to follow up this letter and to inquire as to the possibility of an interview.

Sincerely,

Donald E. Thompson
708/555-3909

JEREMY S. PANDY
1441 S. Goebert
Providence, RI 00231

March 11, 2000

Anderson Publishing Inc.
1000 7th Avenue
Suite 1000
New York, NY 10019
Attn: Delores Darnell
      Director of Personnel

Dear Ms. Darnell:

Through your recent press release, I became aware of the recent departure of your company's president, Myron Strickland. With that in mind, I am forwarding my resume to you for your consideration in your search for a new president.

With over 20 years of experience in the publishing industry, including most currently Vice President of Advertising at Johnson Publishing in Providence, I feel that I have the experience and the industry knowledge to tackle this challenge. My employment history also includes stints with Rebus Publishing and *Time* magazine.

I believe that Anderson Publishing is a company with a future, and I am convinced that I can help shape that future. I expect great things from myself and Anderson.

I will be following up this letter with a telephone call next week. I will be in New York City during the week of March 20 and would be happy to meet with you regarding this position at that time.

Thank you for your kind consideration.

Sincerely,

Jeremy S. Pandy
401/555-1234
401/555-3782

RANDALL KENNEDY • 7901 Martella Ave. • New Orleans, LA 29920

August 23, 2001

Robert Minnelli
President
Dormar Corporation
111 E. State St.
Chicago, IL 60606

Dear Mr. Minnelli:

I am interested in applying for the position of Senior Personnel Administrator at Dormar. I learned of this opening through a mutual friend, Donald Donner, who works in your accounting division. I am enclosing my resume for this reason.

Currently, Johannson, Inc., employs me as Industrial Relations Manager. I oversee all labor relations with the corporation and the union, work with the personnel department to plan labor policy, review hiring practices, and handle many other related functions. Prior to my current position, I served as Assistant Personnel Manager at Target Discount Stores.

My interest in your opening stems from a desire to move more in the direction of personnel administration. I believe that my experience in industrial relations gives me a unique perspective as a personnel administrator.

I will be in the Chicago area from September 2 through September 15. At your convenience, I would like to interview for this position at that time. I will be in touch with you soon.

Sincerely,

Randall Kennedy
504/555-2900
504/555-2810
rbk@earthlink.net

JOHN L. RYDER
211 W. Fourth St. #211
Brooklyn, NY 10001
718/555-8080

June 12, 2001

John Junot
Fidelity Insurance Co.
1440 W. 57th St.
New York, NY 10019

Dear Mr. Junot:

I am responding to your advertisement for a Branch Manager/East Coast for your insurance company. As you asked, I am enclosing my resume and a list of references.

After several years of working as an agent and an adjustor, I am ready to make the move into a management position, and I believe that a position of this kind at Fidelity would benefit both me and the company. My vast experience in the insurance industry has prepared me well for this next step in my career.

Please review my resume and let me know if and when you would like me to come to your office for an interview. I look forward to meeting with you.

Sincerely,

John L. Ryder

August 23, 2001

David Bascombe III
Sears & Roebuck, Inc.
1000 S. Adams
Chicago, IL 60601

Dear Mr. Bascombe:

I am responding to your job listing for a Marketing Management Trainee that was posted in the placement office at Boston University. I am interested in applying for this position, and therefore I am enclosing my resume with this letter.

I have recently graduated from Boston University with a degree in Economics, and I am anxious to find a position in the marketing field. I am currently working toward a Master's in Marketing by taking evening courses.

My work experience includes employment as a Marketing Assistant for Lewis Advertising Agency in Boston and as a Telephone Interviewer for Paterno Marketing.

I will be in the Chicago area the week of September 12. Would it be possible to set up an interview with you during that week? If so, please contact me at your earliest convenience.

Sincerely,

Janis Darien
345 W. 3rd St. #42
Boston, MA 02210
617/555-3291
janis@bostonu.com

10/19/01

Geraldine Powers
Powers & Powers, Inc.
7700 Main St.
Las Vegas, NV 88883

Dear Ms. Powers:

After spending the last four years as an accountant for Hervey & Co., I am ready to pursue a management position in a larger accounting firm such as yours. Powers & Powers' reputation as a leader in the field has led me to write to you regarding possible management opportunities in your company.

At Hervey & Co., I have managed insurance, financial, and brokerage accounting, handled general cost accounting procedures, and designed systems for budget and cash flow accounting. During the past four years, I have developed solid accounting skills. Now I am ready for something more challenging.

I am enclosing my resume. Please contact me regarding any openings appropriate for me.

Sincerely,

Crystal Cartier
1201 E. Maple Drive
Las Vegas, NV 89901

January 14, 2001

Gekko Publishing, Inc.
1700 Avenue of Industry
Dallas, TX 78989
Attn: Ricardo Montoya
       Director of Personnel

Dear Mr. Montoya:

This letter is a response to your advertisement in *Houston Chronicle*'s classified section. The position of assistant manager of operations for a publisher of Gekko's stature is one that appeals to me greatly. I am enclosing my resume for your consideration.

Currently, I am assistant manager for a small but dynamic publisher in Houston, American National Books, Inc. My experience at American National includes orchestrating market analyses, identifying clients' needs and meeting them, maintaining accounts, and establishing new accounts. I also oversee the company's E-commerce on the www.anb.com company website. Previous to this position, I served as a sales representative for Unico International in Dallas.

I am willing to come to Dallas for an interview at your convenience. Coming back to work in Dallas is something I am looking forward to. It's a wonderful city.

Please feel free to contact me at either phone number listed below. I look forward to meeting you and discussing this opportunity.

Sincerely,

Renee Gylkison
8 E. Western Avenue
Houston, TX 75737
713/555-8098
713/555-6000
renee@anb.com

LISA STANSFIELD
14 E. ThreePenny Road
Detroit, MI 33290
313/555-3489

4/18/00

Zan Marketing
500 E. Hubbard Street
Detroit, MI 33909
Attn: Hilda C. Roane

Dear Ms. Roane:

I am interested in applying for your opening for a Marketing Manager at Zan Marketing. I learned of this opening from your ad in the *Detroit Free Press*.

Currently, I am employed as Marketing Director for Seven Eleven, Inc., in Detroit. Some of my accomplishments at this company include the development of a successful marketing campaign, the implementation of marketing strategies to increase sales at less-profitable outlets, and the designing of a training program for store managers and staff.

Zan's positive reputation is well-known throughout the industry, and I am most interested in helping to perpetuate that reputation.

Please feel free to call me for an interview. My resume is enclosed.

Best regards,

Lisa Stansfield

SALLY JOHANSON
3240 Santa Monica Blvd.
Los Angeles, CA 90028

December 20, 2000

David G. Sandler
Director of Human Resources
Nessex Motor Co.
12000 Wilshire Blvd.
Santa Monica, CA 90390

Dear Mr. Sandler:

I am interested in applying for the position of Assistant Manager at your Lexus dealership in Santa Monica. Your ad in the *L.A. Times* alerted me to this opening.

I am currently a sales representative for Pontiac in Los Angeles where I have handled sales, market analyses, research, forecasts, and service and billing problems.

I have held this position for three years and am now ready to explore new challenges in auto sales--assistant manager being one of them. I feel I am qualified for this job.

Enclosed is my resume. Please take me into consideration. I look forward to interviewing with you.

Sincerely,

Sally Johanson
213/555-9832 (Home)
213/555-2121 (Work)

July 22, 2001

Neil Tennant
Director of Human Resources
Parker Thomas Accounting, Inc.
7717 E. 3rd Terrace
Milwaukee, WI 55250

Dear Mr. Tennant:

I am seeking employment in the field of accounting, particularly a position leading to management. Enclosed is my resume.

I am a recent M.B.A. graduate of the University of Wisconsin at Madison. My area of concentration at the university was accounting and my studies included the following:

> Basic, Intermediate, and Advanced Accounting
> Business Law
> Cost Accounting
> Statistical Methods
> Planning and Control
> Tax Law
> Investments

Prior to my graduate degree, I earned a B.A. in History from the University of Chicago, where I graduated Summa Cum Laude and won the Leopold Scholarship.

Considering my preparation, I am ready to begin my career in accounting. I will be contacting you soon regarding possible job openings. Thank you for your time and consideration.

Sincerely,

William Gavin
2666 Western Ave. #44
Madison, WI 55590
608/555-2029

JOHANNA FARAC
152 S. Fedner Drive
Omaha, NE 73802

September 30, 2000

Susan P. Evers
Federated Books, Inc.
1442 S. 7th Avenue
Omaha, NE 73092

Dear Ms. Evers:

I am responding to your ad in *The Omaha Register* for a management trainee for your bookstore. Enclosed is my resume and salary requirements as you requested.

All of my life I have had a fascination with books and bookstores. In high school I worked in the student bookstore all four years, and my work experience includes stints as a salesperson for Fern Books and as assistant sales manager for Crown Books in Omaha.

Thank you for your time and consideration. I look forward to hearing from you and meeting with you soon.

Sincerely,

Johanna Farac
402/555-9000 (Day)
402/555-6712 (Evening)

September 22, 2001

Carlos Castillo
Director of Human Resources
Macy's Inc.
5744 N. Franklin Ave.
Miami, FL 33333

Dear Mr. Castillo:

I am responding to your advertisement for a Senior Audit Manager for your company. The ad requested someone with audit experience in a department store. I have such experience.

For the past nine years, I have served as Audit Manager for Jordan Marsh Company in Ft. Myers, Florida. My responsibilities include overseeing analytical review and verification of financial records, developing audit programs, establishing guidelines for physical distribution of inventory, and evaluation of internal controls. Before Jordan Marsh, I worked for National Textile Co. and Held & Perkins, both in audit and finance.

My resume is enclosed to give you a complete picture of my experience and qualifications. Please review it and contact me if you would like me to come for an interview. I look forward to hearing from you soon.

Sincerely,

Stephanie Shepard
804 N. Victoria Park Rd.
Ft. Myers, FL 30013
941/555-2000 (Work)
941/555-5555 (Home)
rosebud@inet.com

WINONA T. SIMPSON
420 W. Easterly Avenue
Indianapolis, IN 49091

September 2, 2000

Thomas E. Eagletender
Pizza Hut, Inc.
4200 Bolt Avenue
Indianapolis, IN 48902

Dear Mr. Eagletender:

David Porter of your marketing department informed me that you were looking for a new P.R. manager for your Midwest office. Therefore, I am sending my resume for your consideration in regard to this position.

Currently, I serve as P.R. director for Blockbuster Video in Indianapolis, where I have been since 1995. Before that I worked as marketing representative for Jeron Stereo and as P.R. assistant for Kader Advertising.

My accomplishments include developing a successful marketing campaign for Blockbuster, implementing marketing strategies to increase sales at less profitable outlets, designing a training program for store managers and staff, and developing the website.

I believe my resume speaks for itself. I would very much like to meet with you to discuss this position further. Please contact me at 317/555-1212 at your convenience.

Sincerely,

Winona T. Simpson